"Once again Claire nas given us compelling
reasons why we should all be more mindful, through
her glorious evocation of why birds inspire, enthral, and
ultimately calm us. The 20-minute Sit Spot in particular is a
new and entrancing idea that we should all adopt. This little
book is full of good advice: above all, watch, notice
and learn with your heart, not just your mind."

FIONA REYNOLDS
MASTER, EMMANUEL COLLEGE, CAMBRIDGE
FORMER DIRECTOR-GENERAL, NATIONAL TRUST,
AND AUTHOR OF "THE FIGHT FOR BEAUTY"

"At a time when protecting our natural home
is one of our greatest and most urgent challenges,
books like Claire's are critical to inspire us all to take action.
Bird and nature conservation starts with people who love,
care about and value birds and nature. Let this book inspire
you to fall in love with birds and through them
reconnect with the wonders of nature."

PATRICIA ZURITA
CHIEF EXECUTIVE, BIRDLIFE INTERNATIONAL

Mindfulness *in* Bird Watching

Meditations on Nature & Freedom

Claire Thompson

Leaping Hare Press

Quarto

First published in hardback in 2017 as *The Art of Mindful Birdwatching*.

This hardback edition first published in 2024 by Leaping Hare Press,
an imprint of The Quarto Group.
One Triptych Place
London, SE1 9SH,
United Kingdom
T (0)20 7700 6700
www.Quarto.com

A catalogue record for this book is available from the British Library.

ISBN 978-0-7112-9874-3
Ebook ISBN 978-0-7112-9875-0

10 9 8 7 6 5 4 3 2 1

Editorial Director: Monica Perdoni
Designer: Ginny Zeal
Illustrator: Melvyn Evans

Printed in China

CONTENTS

INTRODUCTION

*Who has never gazed enviously at a bird
soaring through the sky? Or delighted in the
uplifting tunes of nature's songsters? Birds are an
everyday source of beauty, wisdom, and wonder.
They're also the ideal inspiration for the practice of
mindfulness. Bird flight is a wonderful symbol of our
freedom to soar through life without constraint, and
mindfulness similarly enables us to invite freedom
into our lives. Bird watching is also the perfect
entry point to rekindle our innate bond
with the natural world.*

DISCOVERING MINDFULNESS
THROUGH BIRD WATCHING

◆

How often do you notice birds? Can you identify different species? Or have you never watched birds before? Rest assured, your experience to date is irrelevant. This book isn't about how much knowledge or expertise we have—it's about wholeheartedly enjoying our encounters with birds.

B IRDS HAVE ALWAYS FASCINATED PEOPLE. Poets, artists, and scientists have forever been inspired by them and the majority of cultures include them in their art, music, and legends. They appear in the mythology of ancient Egypt, where the sacred ibis was venerated as a symbol of the god Thoth; in the Inca and Tiwanaku empires of South America, birds were depicted transgressing the boundaries between the earthly and underground spiritual realms; and birdsong has inspired musicians and composers, such as Vivaldi, Beethoven, and Tchaikovsky. Birds can do wonders for our hearts and minds if we simply give them attention— which is where mindfulness comes in.

I was once walking along the top of beautiful white cliffs on a sunny spring afternoon, enjoying the gentle sea breeze on my face and the scent of the salt-infused air. I stopped and looked out to sea. Four gulls were riding the wind along the cliffs, repeatedly circling out over the waves and back toward the cliff face. They let go, giving in to the air currents, slowly floating up and down. Their flight was effortless and free. I began to follow one of them with my gaze as it was lifted toward the sky on an unexpected updraft. It remained hanging in the air for a moment. The skill of its balancing act was astonishing—continuously adjusting its tilt to remain upright, seemingly weightless, resting on the breeze. As I watched it rise, its pure white body looked radiant against the clear blue sky and sunshine lit up the contours of its graceful silhouette. At one with the wind, it was entirely present. Inspired and a little envious, I was moved to join it and opened my arms out, keeping my gaze on the bird. In that moment, all my thoughts and inhibitions vanished. The gull and I flew together, and the sense of freedom was intoxicating. I felt intensely alive.

They show their pleasure, and shall I do less?
Happier of happy though I be, like them
I cannot take possession of the sky,
Mount with a thoughtless impulse and wheel there
One of a mighty multitude, whose way
And motion is a harmony and dance
Magnificent.

FROM "THE RECLUSE"
WILLIAM WORDSWORTH (1770–1850)

What is Mindfulness?

Mindfulness is paying attention, on purpose, without judging and with kind acceptance, to our thoughts, feelings, bodily sensations, and surrounding environment. Through practicing mindfulness we notice, accept, and directly experience our lives in the present moment. We tend to live a large portion of our lives on autopilot, lost in our thoughts. Mindfulness is about awakening and breaking free from the apparent constraints of our minds, while experiencing life fully.

What is Bird Watching?

There are various terms you may hear used in association with different approaches to "bird watching." In case you're new to the bird-watching world, here's a brief crash course on who's called what and why.

The main terms used are: bird watching, birding, and twitching. "Bird watching" has become the generic term used to describe the act of watching and listening to birds. "Birding" is a term used in relation to bird-watching experts who are well versed in bird identification, with an active pursuit of finding and studying birds. They have knowledge of different species, their habitats, their movements, and how to identify them. "Twitching" refers to birders who actively pursue rare birds

Our bodies and minds are made up of nature's elements. We are nature.

seen by others; they may travel long distances to see them. Some twitchers and birders keep lists of bird species they encounter, lending a competitive edge to the pastime.

This book is addressed to everyone who wants to watch birds, regardless of knowledge, experience, or motivation. For the established bird watchers among you, we'll explore how a more mindful approach can greatly enrich your experience of your favorite hobby. For the beginners, I hope to introduce you to mindfulness while inspiring you to enjoy the incredible diversity of the avian world.

Why Mindfulness & Bird Watching?

Nature is around us and within us always. How would we be here experiencing life if it weren't for our bodies, air, water, the sun, and the sky? The simple answer is that we wouldn't. Nature gives rise to all life, including our own. Our bodies and minds originated in the natural world and are made up of nature's elements. We are nature.

The problem is that in our modern lives, we often forget our innate bond with the natural world. We've started to lose touch with the rest of nature as our lives have become increasingly urban and are spent mostly indoors. In fact, many of us hardly spend any time in nature at all. Neglecting this bond is the root cause of much of the world's suffering. It's having dramatic consequences for our well-being and is the primary cause of the current global environmental crisis.

I am passionate about life and believe that a greater awareness of life around us and within us is the secret to greater happiness, peace, and contentment. Birds are one of the few groups of animals in the natural world that are always present wherever we are across the entire globe. We share our everyday lives with them, so paying attention to them doesn't require a huge change in what we do or how we live. Bird watching is thus a wonderful entry point for rekindling our innate connection with our natural home.

Bird watching is also the ideal activity to combine with the practice of mindfulness. Due to the amazing diversity in the avian world, there are infinite numbers of things to appreciate about birds. They are beautiful, funny, fascinating, surprising, mysterious, and awe-inspiring. They also have a great deal to teach us about mindfulness, happiness, and life itself. Being mindful of birds will only invite more beauty, fun, and wisdom into our lives.

An Invitation to Fly

Our experience of bird watching varies, depending on where we are, with different habitats offering opportunities to discover new aspects of mindfulness. Mindful bird watching isn't about birds in isolation—instead it's about our meetings with them in unique moments and circumstances. I invite you to join me on a journey—starting at home and moving through open country, forests, coasts, and mountains—to experience birds while at the same time gaining greater insight into the practice of mindfulness. All you need is your body, an open heart, and an open mind.

This book is an invitation to enjoy the magnificent diversity of colors, songs, flight patterns, and behaviors displayed by birds. It's a guide to noticing them, exploring how they make us feel, and discovering what we can learn from them.

Our dream of flight is as old as humankind itself. Haven't we all at some point wished that we could fly? Inspired by bird flight, we have invented hot-air balloons, gliders, and airplanes. However, it's unlikely we'll ever grow wings! If our desire to fly comes from a yearning for freedom, experiencing new perspectives, and living without constraint, then perhaps mindful bird watching is a good compromise. Why not let birds inspire us to soar through our lives with greater freedom and happiness?

DO I NEED BINOCULARS?

Although not essential, a basic pair of binoculars can take you closer to birds without disturbing them while increasing your intimacy with them. They will make it easier to identify differences between birds so that you can get to know individuals. Notice their colors. Notice any distinctive patterns on their plumage. Watch out for the subtle twitches in their bodies as they breathe and move. The stunning red face and yellow wing patch of a goldfinch look even more vibrant close up.

CHAPTER ONE

MEET THE BIRDS

*Birds have been part of our lives for
millennia. Like us, they're part of nature.
They're always around us, wherever we are. Our
yards, towns, and cities are the perfect places to begin
our mindful bird-watching journey. Here, birds are our
inspiration to practice mindfulness, with a particular
focus on nurturing compassion and rekindling our
beginner's mind. Connecting with birds and nature
in our everyday lives is not only essential for our
well-being, but also provides the opportunity for
us to experience a true sense of comfort
and belonging.*

MINDFUL MEETINGS WITH BIRDS

❖

It's time to meet the birds, and you can begin without even leaving your house. "Window bird watching" is the ideal exercise to enjoy while eating breakfast or taking a break from daily chores.

AS I SIT HERE, WRITING ON A COLD winter's afternoon, I need only turn my head to look out of my window to see a blackbird, a robin, a great tit, and a wren. The blackbird, with striking bright orange rings around its eyes, is pecking for worms. In the corner of the yard, the red-breasted robin is perched on top of a bush. In the tree, the great tit catches my eye with its neat black mask and white cheeks as it hops from branch to branch. And the tiny wren is skipping furtively among the ivy looking for insects. If I listen carefully, even with the window closed, I can hear the great tit's whistled calls and the robin's winter song. Birds share our lives.

Why not try "window bird watching" yourself? Look out of the window. Pay attention for a few minutes. What can you see and hear? Whether up in the sky, down on the ground, or in a nearby tree, you will almost certainly see a bird or two.

There's no requirement to be able to identify the various species you see. Although it can enhance your bird-watching experience, this book will focus on guiding you through being curious, paying attention, and enjoying what you notice, reigniting a sense of wonder. This is the essence of mindfulness.

Rediscovering Mindfulness

Let's begin with a simple exercise. Find a quiet place to sit for a few minutes. Start by noticing where you feel your breath. Do you feel it in your nostrils? Your chest? Your abdomen? Notice where your body touches the ground. Are you experiencing any physical sensations or emotions? Notice any thoughts you have. Become aware of what's around you. What can you see? Hear? Smell? Touch? Taste? Just notice what you encounter without seeking to label it or achieve anything in particular. Noticing our experience in this way is the first component of mindfulness.

Mindfulness is something we do. It isn't a concept, an idea, or a belief. What's more, we all experience it already—it's our natural state prior to the accumulation of social and environmental conditioning. Mindfulness is less about learning a new skill and more about rediscovering one we already have that has fallen into disuse. Like the sun hidden by clouds, this awareness is always shining, no matter what we're experiencing.

The sun rises, the sun falls, the wind
blows and the birds sing no matter where you are.
These are experiences that unite us all . . .
something we can all enjoy together.

FROM "FIVE BIRDS ON A WIRE"
MELANIE CHARLENE

How We Notice

The second component of mindfulness is *how* we notice. Mindfulness is usually defined as paying attention, on purpose and *nonjudgmentally,* to our thoughts, feelings, bodily sensations, and surrounding environment. How we do this involves infusing our awareness with a particular set of "colors" or attitudes. It's like cultivating a flower border, which flourishes when a set of elements are present, such as water, nutrients, and light. The nonjudgmental part of mindfulness is about observing and kindly welcoming our direct experience as it is, without seeking to change it. Left unchecked, our narrating minds automatically judge and label our experiences of life. Mindfulness is learning to be aware of these judgments, taking a step back and keeping an open mind.

It's important to note that developing mindfulness, although accessible to us all, requires practice. Practice every day; the more you practice, the more mindful you'll become.

Bringing Mindfulness to Bird Watching

One of my friends has been an avid bird watcher since childhood. He can recognize most of the different types of birds he comes across by sight or sound. When out walking with him, I'm frequently impressed by his ability to name bird species with unwavering confidence. "Reed bunting! Sedge warbler! Chiffchaff!" In fact, I've acquired much of my own knowledge of birds and their ecology from him.

MINDFULNESS EXERCISE

MINDFULNESS OF BREATH

By bringing our awareness to our breath, we can train ourselves to become grounded in the present moment. Find a quiet place to sit, close your eyes, and bring your awareness to where you feel your breath. Observe any sensations, experiencing each breath as it happens without seeking to change it. Follow the sensations as the air comes into your body and goes out again. Your mind will wander, which is perfectly normal. When you notice this, recognize any thoughts arising and bring your attention back to the sensations of the breath. This noticing is a moment of mindfulness. If you have to bring your mind back a million times, simply do so, with kindness. You can practice this exercise for just a few minutes or for longer periods—but remember to practice regularly, ideally once a day.

Nevertheless, I became increasingly struck by how rarely he stopped to really watch, listen to, or get to know the birds we encountered. One day I asked him: "Why don't you ever stop and watch blue tits, they're gorgeous birds!" He replied: "Of course they are, but I see them all the time." Saddened by the fact that he no longer felt the enchantment in watching these characterful blue-and-yellow gems, I later mentioned mindfulness to him. Over the subsequent years, this helped revive his original passion for bird watching.

Watching Birds with Our Hearts

Mindful bird watching is setting aside knowledge, labels, and expectations while paying full attention—moment by moment and nonjudgmentally—to our direct experience of birds. It doesn't depend on having special equipment or particular skills. It's simply looking, listening, and being curious about life. It's developing a habit of really noticing birds—their colors, their sounds, their flight patterns, and their behaviors. It's becoming aware of how watching and listening to them makes us feel. Moreover, being mindful increases the quality and frequency of our encounters with birds. In essence, mindful bird watching is best described as watching birds with our hearts instead of our minds. Let's remember that meeting a bird is a precious moment of connection with one of our most familiar natural relatives.

THE BENEFITS OF MINDFULNESS

Research has shown that regular mindfulness practice results in physical changes in the brain, which lead to:

- Increased concentration
- Increased creativity
- Increased vitality
- Reduced stress and anxiety
- Better overall physical and emotional well-being
- Better sleep.

OUR NATURAL FAMILY

◆

The one thing we have in common with all other life forms is that we share the same home, which we call nature. Our bodies and minds evolved in the natural world and are made of nature's elements. In fact, we are nature.

I'VE ALWAYS FOUND A GREAT SENSE OF COMFORT and belonging in the knowledge that all living things are part of the same family. In *On the Origin of Species*, Charles Darwin called this family "The great Tree of Life." It never ceases to amaze me that from the smallest bacteria, to the tallest trees to the birds in our yards, we're all related, descended from a common ancestor, which came to life 3.8 billion years ago—with our species, *Homo sapiens*, evolving 200,000 years ago.

So where do our feathered relatives fit in to this tree? They probably descended from flying dinosaurs around 150 million years ago. Since then, more than 10,000 different species of birds have branched out in this great Tree of Life, giving rise to the awe-inspiring diversity of colors, shapes, sizes, and behaviors that now surround us. We're thus directly connected to birds through our natural family bond.

The problem is that we've forgotten this; we live our lives as if we were separate from nature. Why has this happened? It has something to do with the evolution of our incredible ability for conscious, abstract thought. We've invested much time and energy in developing our minds—creating theories, beliefs and concepts—while losing touch with our bodies and with direct sensory experience. Our lives have become much more urban and indoors, with many of us nowadays spending hardly any time in nature at all. Not only is neglecting our innate bond with the natural world having serious consequences for our health and well-being—often known as nature-deficit disorder—but it's also one of the causes of the global environmental crisis. How will we be inspired to love and protect the natural world we depend on if we have no direct experience of it? Unsurprisingly, our belonging in the natural world means that experiencing it is vital to us and to the rest of life with which we share the planet, and nature has a lot to teach us about how to lead happier, wiser lives.

It's time to bring our awareness back to the natural world. The practice of mindfulness is the exploration and appreciation of our experience of life within us and around us—and where better to explore life than in nature? Our most familiar natural relatives—the birds—are the ideal entry point to reconnecting with our natural home.

◆

Too much energy in your country is
spent developing the mind instead of the heart.

FROM "NEVER GIVE UP"
DALAI LAMA XIV

◆

An Invitation to Your Yard

◆

Let's start by inviting birds into our backyards—the easiest place for us to get acquainted with them, when they become regular visitors. These birds will gift us with comfort, joy, and humor on a daily basis.

W E CAN ALL WELCOME BIRDS into our homes; not only is it the best place to get to know them but also the perfect context within which to begin to hone our mindfulness skills, including developing our compassionate mind. So what are you waiting for? Invite the birds around.

The easiest way to do so is to provide food and shelter for them. You can immediately give them food by setting up a feeder. However, if you're able to, you can also make sure that natural food sources are available to them by planting bird-friendly berry bushes, fruit trees, and flowering plants that produce nutritious seed heads. Prickly bushes and thick climbers will make sure your visitors have safe nesting sites and secure cover from predators. Be patient; it may take a little time for the birds to discover their new local haven, but you can be sure you'll soon be hosting your first guest.

The First of Many

I remember vividly the joy I experienced when my first guest, a delightful blue tit, landed on my bird feeder. What a privilege to be visited by such a delicate, agile, and attractive wild creature. I gazed at it as it pecked at the seeds, continuously tilting its tiny head skyward, timid yet boldly alert. I couldn't take my eyes off its vivid blue cap and white halo. Full of excitement, I could have watched this puffed-up little jewel forever. But this wasn't to be, because it flitted off after a few seconds, disappearing into the neighbor's yard. My initial feeling of frustration for my loss was soon replaced by a deep sense of gratitude for having spent these few short moments watching this exquisite little bird from my home. Whoever your first visitor may be, really take pleasure in this unique moment of connection with the wild. From then onward, you'll be sure to welcome many more.

SETTING UP A BIRD FEEDER

Birds will visit our yards if their basic needs are catered for. Here are a few tips:

- Make sure you can see your feeder from a window—you want to be able to enjoy your guests' company.
- Hang your feeder out of the wind and away from windows to avoid collisions.
- Don't hang your feeder too close to tree trunks, bushes, or fences, which may hide seed-munching squirrels and bird-hungry cats.
- Make sure there's cover and shelter for birds to rest in between feeding trips or to escape to as a refuge from a passing hawk.
- To make your feeder even more enticing, you could place a birdbath nearby for drinking and bathing.

Set aside some time to get to know your backyard birds. Notice their colors. Pay attention to the patterns on their feathers. Observe their movements—the subtle twitches of their bodies as they breathe, the vibration of their throats when they sing, and their skillful removal of the husks from seeds with their beaks. Become aware of the patterns and speeds of their gaits, the life in their eyes, and the focused intent in their behaviors. Notice how they fly. Do you notice any interactions between individuals? Are some birds bolder or shyer than others? If your mind begins to wander as you do this, don't worry. It's what our minds do out of habit, all the time. Just bring your attention kindly back to the birds.

Becoming familiar with backyard birds also involves tuning into their songs. Sit in your yard and close your eyes. Listen to the calls and songs you can hear. Are they high- or low-pitched? Can you recognize any tunes or phrases? Notice how you feel—what thoughts come to mind? Simply notice, without judgment, and appreciate the richness of life around you.

The Diversity of Life

To borrow Darwin's words, nature comes in "endless forms most beautiful and most wonderful." Life depends on diversity, with every species demonstrating another ingenious solution to the challenge of survival. As you get to know your backyard visitors, you'll soon begin to distinguish different species. Although this book won't focus on their identification, learning to recognize them can be a true celebration of the glorious variety of life. Moreover, using their names is the easiest way to share our love of birds with others. How would I have written this book without using species names? Names help us to communicate and understand the world around us. So when you discover a species you haven't come across before, why not find out what it's called? Watch carefully, listen attentively, and look them up in a field guide. It's that simple, and it's how every bird watcher learns.

INSPIRED BY LIFE

◆

Watching backyard birds is an infinite source of aliveness, reassurance, comfort, beauty, respect, and humility. It's an opportunity to gain insight into the many different facets of life itself and an inspiration to feel truly part of our beautiful natural world.

A FEW WEEKS AGO, FEELING particularly tired, I decided to spend some time with the birds in my yard one morning. I was immediately absorbed by the frenzy of activity on and around my bird feeder. A robin hopped from perch to perch around it—playfully enjoying its breakfast from various vantage points. As it flew off, a great tit immediately popped in for a few pecks. This smart and colorful black-hooded bird then hopped onto a nearby branch, against which it cleaned its beak. The coast was now clear for a blue tit to dash in for a

---

There is an unreasonable joy to be had
from the observation of small birds going
about their bright, oblivious business.

FROM "THE COMPLETE LACHLAN"
GRANT HUTCHISON

---

quick seed or two until it was chased off by the great tit. Next, a chaffinch, with its smoky gray cap and black-and-white wings, paid its morning visit. His departure was the opportunity that a tiny coal tit, a shy black-masked bird, had been waiting for. His fleeting visit allowed for him to snatch just a single seed before he was on his way. The speed with which they all came and went was captivating. All of them were intensely present, alert, and alive. No energy could be wasted when life was at stake; feeding is a serious business. Their liveliness and purpose were infectious—inspiring me to make the most of the day ahead.

A Friend's Familiar Melody

Our garden backyard can also provide us with comfort and reassurance amid the challenges of daily life. I recently came home from work feeling frustrated and tense. As I sat down with a cup of tea, I heard the rich, uplifting tune of the resident blackbird in my yard singing his familiar melody, which I had grown to know over the spring months. I peered

---

◆

I value my garden more for being full of blackbirds than of
cherries, and very frankly give them fruit for their songs.

FROM "THE SPECTATOR"
JOSEPH ADDISON (1672–1719)

◆

---

out of the window and there he was on the branch he perches
on every evening. His sole purpose was to broadcast his
beautiful song to the neighborhood for a couple more hours
as dusk fell. It was heartening to know that despite my state of
mind, this little fellow continued to sing his fruity tune, as he
did each spring evening. I felt grateful to him for reminding
me that whatever we're experiencing, life continues moment
by moment—and there's always time for another song.

Celebrating Beauty

Beauty is good for us; it lifts our spirits and inspires our deep
admiration for the world around us. Once we begin to pay
attention, we realize that it's everywhere—and the avian
world is no exception. A few years ago, I visited a friend in
Mexico who owns a house in the mountains with a tropical
garden. Nectar feeders, ten of them, provided the attraction
for countless hummingbirds—iridescent jewels of dizzying
movement and hyperactivity. Hundreds of them were darting
back and forth, their tiny wings buzzing with a myriad of brilliant colors flashing intermittently in the sunlight. I was

transfixed by their dazzling fragility, posturing, and jostling with each other for space to feed, while emitting their characteristic "zitting" calls—a cameo of the avian world in all its vibrant glory. Of course, our regular backyard birds are no less alluring. Wherever we live in the world, the colors and songs of the birds we see every day display incredible beauty.

Undeniable Realities

Bird watching can be comforting and beautiful, but let's not forget that watching birds is watching life, and life isn't always pleasurable. There's a common misconception that mindfulness equates to blissful, thoughtless relaxation. This is not so. Mindfulness is welcoming all our experiences of life, whether pleasant, painful, or neutral, and mindful bird watching enables us to gain insight into the undeniable realities of living.

A rustling in the shrubs once caught my attention while I was relaxing in my yard. An awesome backyard-bird predator revealed itself: a sparrow hawk. I took a closer look with my binoculars, and was astonished to discover that this proud, bright orange-eyed creature had caught a wood pigeon. Given the size and weight of the pigeon, the hawk couldn't carry it off to feast on it in peace. Instead, I watched it sit over its prey, tearing off gory morsels until its crop was bulging. The bird stared straight back at me, fiercely protective of its catch. After a few minutes and with a full crop, it flew off to finish digesting its mighty meal elsewhere.

I felt sadness and empathy for the helpless pigeon, yet simultaneously great admiration and respect for the magnificent hawk. The bird's impressive predatory skills had earned it a well-deserved meal. In that moment, I was reminded that all living things live and die. It seemed wrong, unfair, and cruel, but this was merely my mind's judgment. Eventually, I settled into a gentle acceptance of this reality of raw nature— concurrently beautiful and ruthless.

Intimate Moments

Chance encounters with wild animals can offer us some of our most humbling experiences and backyard bird watching gifts us with daily opportunities for these meetings. You may also witness intimate moments between individuals.

Last year, a pair of robins had built a nest in the ivy-covered fence in my parents' yard. On various occasions in early spring, we watched them courting—feeding each other with great dedication. The female solicited food from the male by uttering short, monosyllabic calls as she lowered her quivering wings. Later in the season, we watched them feeding their hatched chicks: one parent alert and guarding the nest, the other carrying food back. It was an immense privilege to see the pair unite to nurture these fragile new lives. The intimacy we can experience when bird watching at home is the perfect opportunity for us to connect with birds as individual sentient beings, through the development of compassion.

COMPASSION FOR SENTIENT INDIVIDUALS

◆

Just like us, birds are alive and their lives inherently deserve respect. They, too, are individual sentient beings; their experience of life may be different from our own, but it is no less worthy.

HAVE YOU CONSIDERED THAT EVERY BIRD is a unique individual going about its life? The more familiar we become with birds, the more likely we will be to begin to dismiss individual birds of a species we've seen before. "Why stop and look at this one? It's just another blackbird!" But when you met your first human being, did you assume that you had met them all? Why should it be different for birds? Every encounter is with a potentially different bird, another life.

Thinking of birds as individuals can be challenging, because we are addicted to novelty. Seeing a rare bird you've never encountered before is more of a thrill than seeing another house sparrow in

Chance encounters with birds can offer us some of our most humbling experiences.

your yard. But in reality, each house sparrow is unique and each meeting is special. Our bird-watching experiences depend on the individual bird, what it's doing, its location, the time of day, and our state of mind. Through watching birds more mindfully, we can transform the ordinary into the extraordinary each time we come across one of our feathered relatives.

Rupert the Robin

So what's the difference between that American goldfinch with the yellow, white and black head and that other American goldfinch you can see with the yellow, white and black head? It's not easy for us to pick up on the physical and behavioral differences between birds of the same species. The distinction is, of course, much more obvious to the birds themselves. Adults must find the right partner, young birds need to recognize their parents, and social birds, such as sparrows, require an awareness of hierarchies within their colonies. In the same way that we recognize each other's faces, voices, and behaviors, birds have evolved to use sight, sound, and touch cues, such as colorful plumage, complex songs, and tactile rituals to recognize their peers. Many perform elaborate courtship dances that enable them to find and recognize their partners during the breeding season. Birds are tuned into the cues of their avian world, just as we are to those of our human world.

Although we'll never be able to see the world through their eyes, this doesn't need to stop us from engaging with birds as individual lives. We can even learn to recognize them. It just takes mindful attention and daily practice. Their size, feather patterns, colors, songs, and behaviors will all display subtly different features. We can even give them names. I've come to know one of the resident robins who visits my yard as Rupert. He's the slightly smaller, shyer, duller-colored robin that typically perches on the back fence. Now that I

And from Humming-Bird to Eagle,

the daily existence of every bird is a remote

and bewitching mystery.

FROM "OUTDOOR PAPERS"
THOMAS WENTWORTH HIGGINSON (1823–1911)

---

recognize him, Rupert has become a friend. Getting to know birds as individuals not only adds intimacy to our relationships with them but also reminds us to stay mindful. That moment when you recognized George the goldfinch as he perched on the tree in your yard, in that luminous orange evening light, is one to savor.

Sentient Beings

How might birds be experiencing the world? Biologists and nature conservationists study birds as biological organisms, seeking to understand their physiology, ecology, distribution, and behaviors. We've always been fascinated by the natural world, and growing our understanding of it through science is a fascinating, commendable, and necessary pursuit. It satisfies our infinite human curiosity, and it is crucial if we are to protect the planet and the species we share it with. However, reducing our relationship with birds to one of scientific rationality can sometimes diminish our humanity, as well as the vitality of the birds themselves. Let's not forget that birds are alive.

Birds have often been considered by scientists to be predictable "stimulus-response" machines, but there's a lot of recent research that reveals that this is not the case. If we open our hearts and minds, we will appreciate that they can be characterful, skillful, innovative, mysterious, and, at times, playful. For instance, crows have been spotted in the snow, improvising their own winter sports, repeatedly sledding down house roofs and car windshields. Other birds, such as pigeons and jays, are known for their outstanding memory and spatial awareness, and crows, vultures, and parrots are able to use tools, including probes made out of twigs and wood to catch or impale larvae as well as stones to crack open eggs to feed on. In this way, they can obtain food that is otherwise difficult to access.

BIRD INTELLIGENCE

Some birds have been found to be significantly cleverer than we ever thought. Parrots are already well-known for their ability to mimic human speech, but corvids, in particular—crows, ravens, rooks, jackdaws, jays, and magpies—have recently astonished scientists with their incredible intelligence. These birds have an enlarged part of their brain, analogous to our neocortex (the part of our brain involved in spatial reasoning, conscious thought, and language), and their intelligence has been suggested to rival that of chimpanzees.

What Might Their Experience Be?

It's important to clarify that engaging with birds as sentient beings does not equate to anthropomorphism. In fact, it's the opposite. Anthropomorphism is the attribution of human characteristics or behaviors to other animals. Instead, in mindful bird watching, we let go of our human perspective and open up to the possibility that birds may have their own experience of life. Why not occasionally take a few moments to wonder what their experience might be? Although we'll never know the answer, imagining what life may feel like from their perspective is a way to nurture our appreciation of them and an opportunity to cultivate our compassionate mind.

COMPASSION

◆

Compassion is an essential part of the practice of mindfulness. When it comes to watching birds, the development of compassion becomes natural and effortless. This is unsurprising, because we are innately connected to birds through our natural family.

I RECENTLY WATCHED A HEDGE SPARROW discreetly collecting small twigs and moss in my back yard. It made various trips back and forth across the lawn and along the shrubs— searching for the perfect materials to construct a nest in which to lay its eggs and raise its young. I was full of admiration for the effort and patience that such a humble creature was putting into the job. I was also aware that, even after all the bird's hard work, success isn't guaranteed in the wild. In that moment, I was overcome by a deep sense of well-wishing toward it. I didn't know what it was like to be in the hedge sparrow's position, or how difficult it was finding its task. Nevertheless, I felt genuine warmth and concern toward it— it deserved to build its nest, lay its eggs, and find enough food to raise its chicks.

This is what we call compassion—one of the main attitudes we infuse our attention with when practicing mindfulness. The clinical psychologist Dr. Paul Gilbert defines compassion as "sensitivity to suffering in self and others with a commitment to try to alleviate and prevent it." We all experience compassion; it's a natural feeling.

As we nurture our compassionate mind, we can extend warmth and well-wishing toward others.

Ancestrally, it ensured the love between mother and child—and enabled us to form close, caring social bonds with friends and family. Compassion is thus good for us, giving rise to feelings of safety, belonging, and connection. Research has shown that it makes us happier and healthier and facilitates more fulfilling relationships with others. Moreover, a compassionate attitude leads to compassionate acts. Wouldn't the world be a better place if we were all a little more compassionate?

So why not exercise our compassion "muscles?" The cultivation of compassion is, in fact, a popular form of Buddhist meditation. When practicing compassion, we begin with ourselves. Normally, we forget to be kind toward ourselves, often beating ourselves up when we fail, make mistakes, or when things don't turn out as we hope. Self-compassion isn't selfish; it's necessary. How can we be kind, warm, and accepting toward others if we treat ourselves harshly? As we nurture our compassionate mind, we can extend this warmth and well-wishing toward other people and life forms. Remember that cultivating compassion requires time and practice.

Compassion in Bird Watching

What about compassionate bird watching? How can we be sensitive to birds' suffering if we don't know what they feel? Ultimately, it's irrelevant. What matters is our attitude, which dictates the actions we take. Compassion is the acknowledgment that all living beings (whether conscious of it or not) want to live, be healthy, and do what they are born to do while enduring the least suffering possible. Birds are living, sentient beings. They need to fly, find food, defend territories, seek partners, build nests, raise young, avoid predators, and, in some cases, travel huge distances on awe-inspiring annual migrations—survival is a tough job. We can help birds along by hanging up bird feeders, maintaining wildlife-friendly yards, making sure we don't disturb them,

MINDFULNESS EXERCISE

WISHING THEM WELL

Find somewhere at your window, in your yard, or in a city where you can watch an individual bird. Bring your attention to your breathing and then to the area where your heart is. Gather a sense of friendliness and compassion there—perhaps by bringing a close friend to mind and wishing them well. Then bring your attention back to the bird. Remind yourself that it's an individual living being like you, going about its life. It's alive and wants to avoid suffering. What challenges might it be facing today? What might it be feeling? What might it need in this moment? You will never know the answers, but it doesn't matter—it's your intention that counts. Wish the bird well by saying to yourself: "May she be well, may she be happy, may she be free from suffering."

and protecting our shared natural home—including the yards, open country, forests, coasts, and mountains that birds also depend on to sustain their lives. Like us, birds have the right to life on the earth. Compassionate bird watching isn't difficult; we are innately connected to our winged relatives as we are to the rest of nature. As you continue to experience the joy, beauty, and wisdom that birds can bring to your day-to-day life, let your love and care for them grow. As you do so, developing compassion toward them will become almost effortless.

CITY SIGHTS & SONGS

◆

Cities can be noisy and busy, and we're often so immersed in our urban worlds and concerns that we fail to notice the natural beauty around us. Yet here, too, we will find ourselves in the company of birds. Why not invite more beauty into our city lives?

I RECALL THE FIRST TIME I DECIDED to walk to work one winter morning with the intention of noticing all the birds I could see or hear. The moment I stepped out of the front door, I tuned into the chorus of birdsong. I was enchanted by the medley of tweets, whistles, chirps, and chatters from close by and afar. As I walked down the street, I met one of the local headline performers: a robin, passionately singing from the top of a tall fence, his red breast visibly vibrating against the azure blue sky behind him. I noticed four black-headed gulls flying over. In the trees, pigeons and doves were quietly perched, dotted around the parking lot, as if they hadn't yet managed to begin their daily business.

I wandered onto the street and caught a glimpse of two acrobatic blue tits moving briskly from branch to branch in a tree in the opposite yard. As I walked on down toward the river, I came across whistling starlings and heard the sudden clucking outbursts of blackbirds as they nervously crossed from yard to yard. I stopped on the bridge and watched a swan preening on the river. The golden winter sunlight shimmered on its white neck as it glided on the water. At the same time, the bright yellow and red beak of a moorhen appeared, poking its head up from behind the reeds.

I couldn't believe how many times I'd walked this route completely unaware, because I'd been thinking of other things, without noticing a single bird. It was as if I'd discovered a whole new world. Next time you're walking through a town or city, set yourself the intention of noticing all the birds you meet on your way. You'll be sure to delight in many sights and sounds you've never experienced before. Discovering new worlds in familiar places is what mindfulness is all about.

Look Up!

Next time you're walking through a town or city, pay attention to your posture. In our modern lives, we tend to walk eyes down, lost in thought, or looking at our cell phones. Looking down can encourage unpleasant states of mind, such as worry, sadness, lack of confidence, or fear. Why not look up? Looking up welcomes positivity and hope into our experience. Look at the sky. What birds do you see? You may see pigeons, sparrow hawks, gulls, buzzards, swifts, swallows,

Why not look up?
Looking up welcomes positivity
and hope into our experience.

and even peregrine falcons. Notice how they make you feel. Follow them with your gaze and let their flight inspire you to be present here and now.

One summer evening, I was walking home from work past a long traffic jam. Drivers were angry and irritated, repeatedly sounding their horns—one of the city noises I dislike the most. Although not driving myself, I began to feel agitated and unnerved. I then remembered one of my favorite mantras: "Look up!" I stopped and turned my eyes to the sky. In an instant, my world was transformed. It turned from being an aggressive assault on my senses to the most astonishing display of skill and beauty. Above the frenzied commotion surrounding me, eight to ten swifts were excitedly careering in a synchronous flock through the sky, screaming as they went. For a moment, I lost myself in the mesmerizing exaltation of their flight as the reverberating sound of the traffic around me faded into the background. I had momentarily flown with the swifts.

Coming Together in the Park

What better place to go on a sunny afternoon than to your local park for a chance to walk in a green space or to sit in the sun reading a book? Urban parks are a charming coming together of people and nature. In our yards, birds are our guests, whereas parks are a shared space; here, we interact with our feathered companions as equals.

In spring, London's St James's Park sees a daily meeting of birds and people. Couples, families, and friends gather around the lakes, talking and watching the ducks, geese, pigeons, and swans. As I walked through the park one Saturday afternoon, it was a delight to stand by the lakes amid people of all ages, enjoying their encounters with birds. An elderly couple marveled at the stunning colors displayed by a mandarin duck. A mother smiled as she watched her spellbound daughters captivated by five adorable recently hatched ducklings. A group of friends were taking photos of a black swan, a bird they had never come across before.

I found myself surrounded by a large flock of cooing pigeons, pecking at food left by picnickers. Pigeons are often dismissed as uninteresting common birds, yet I became completely absorbed by their constant activity—captivated by the interactions between them. Males were fighting off other males; small groups of birds were jostling for food; shyer birds backed off when the bolder characters stepped in. I was amused by the sight of one particular male persistently chasing a seemingly unresponsive female.

My attention was then drawn to a little girl, no more than five or six years old, slowly walking toward one of the lakes. I watched her as she cautiously put her arm out to feed the mallards, her expression a mix of apprehension, curiosity, and friendliness. It was not long before one of the ducks rushed over and snatched the food from her hand. Instantly, her face lit up with a beaming coy smile as she peered back at her parents sitting on a nearby bench, tentatively seeking praise for her act of bravery. She then turned back to watch the mallard, her eyes wide with absolute wonder. I was almost envious of her spontaneous enchantment—the perfect inspiration for rekindling our "beginner's mind."

BEGINNER'S MIND

◆

When we're born, a simple, unadulterated awareness peers out, alert, curious, and full of appreciation for the beauty of the world. When we wake up each morning, this same unconditioned awareness greets the day before concerns, worries, and plans rush in and obscure it.

THE PROBLEM IS THAT AS WE GROW UP, we're conditioned to filter our experience of the world through our knowledge, memories, and judgments—losing a large part of our playful, spontaneous curiosity around life's mysteries. Considering each moment as a new opportunity to discover and open up to possibilities that may challenge our current knowledge and expectations is what we call maintaining a "beginner's mind." Cultivating a beginner's mind is another key part of the practice of mindfulness.

Cultivating a beginner's mind is a key part of the practice of mindfulness.

This childlike attitude makes life so much fresher, more fun, and more engaging; all it requires is practice. Occasionally, set aside your opinions, knowledge, and cherished beliefs. Take some time out from knowing the answer. You don't need to be right. You don't need to understand. Give yourself permission to simply enjoy your experience. Be playful. Daydream and let yourself wonder. Delight in the mystery of questions. In the grand scheme of things, we know little about the world, and anything is possible.

ANYTHING IS POSSIBLE

There's a concept in Zen Buddhism known as *shoshin*, which means "beginner's mind." Shoshin refers to the idea of letting go of your preconceptions and having an attitude of openness. When you're a beginner, your mind is empty and open. You're willing to learn and consider all information, like a child discovering something for the first time. As you develop expertise, your mind becomes less open to new information. What if we cultivated an attitude where everything is possible? Try these tips to rediscover your beginner's mind:

- Disregard common sense.
- Discard fear of failure.
- Be inquisitive.
- Focus on questions instead of answers.
- Don't prejudge—experience life with an open mind.
- Step back, observe, and listen; there's no need to contribute.
- Accept that you don't always need to be right.
- Have fun!

In the beginner's mind there are many possibilities,

but in the expert's there are few.

FROM "ZEN MIND, BEGINNER'S MIND:
INFORMAL TALKS ON ZEN MEDITATION AND PRACTICE"
SHUNRYU SUZUKI (1904–1971)

Fascinated by Life

Birds have forever had a mystical hold over people. They naturally inspire and fascinate us and thus are our perfect companions for rediscovering our beginner's mind. Indeed, they provide us with one of the most exciting ways to connect with the natural world. Endless questions will begin to emerge in our minds once we start paying attention. Why is the robin at my feeder? Where did it come from? Where is it going? Birds give us wings—they are a revitalizing connection to natural life and to the wild. As they reach across all barriers, they are always there to reignite our human sense of hope, wonder, and possibility.

Embrace the thrill of spotting that first guest on the bird feeder in your yard, immerse yourself in the comfort you get from hearing the blackbird's familiar tune, celebrate the awesome colors of dazzling hummingbirds, and let yourself fly with the swifts. This is mindful bird watching. Ultimately, it's just about enjoying the unfathomable natural mystery that we call life.

CHAPTER TWO

COMING TO
OUR SENSES

*Mindful bird watching involves noticing,
seeing, and hearing birds. The more in touch
with our senses we are, the more mindful we'll
become and the richer our bird-watching experiences
will be. Now that we're acquainted with birds at home,
it's time to get outdoors into wilder surroundings.
Being mindful of our senses is essential for our well-
being, and our bodies are our first port of call in the
practice of mindfulness. The huge diversity of
landscapes found in open country and forests
makes them fantastic sensory playgrounds.*

ALL EYES & EARS

◆

Experiencing nature is vital for mind and body, so the next time you have a spare few hours, why not escape to the country and enjoy the tranquillity of the natural world? It's ideal for watching birds.

I LOVE LONG WALKS IN THE COUNTRYSIDE—wandering through woodlands and forests, walking across fields and meadows, and sitting by lakes and streams. I feel invigorated by the wind, the scents of flowers, and the infinite variety of colors and shapes around me. I feel calmed by the sounds of the breeze in the trees, the rustling of reeds, and the buzzing of insects. This gentle, natural stimulation of our senses is the best antidote to the speed and chaotic bustle of modern life.

The incredible diversity of life found in open country and forests makes them marvelous places for us to reconnect with our senses. Our sight, hearing, smell, touch, and taste allow for us to take in the world and experience our lives. Bird watching relies heavily on their use, with a particular emphasis on our eyes and ears. How will we notice birds if we don't listen and look attentively? Seeing them depends on us becoming finely tuned sensory detectives. The sound of leaves rustling, a glimpse of movement in the bushes, or a flash of color between trees are often our only clues that a bird is close by, so we need to be "all eyes and ears." There's no need for expertise; all it takes is for us to reengage with our bodies.

Reconnecting with Nature

Our bodies are our ultimate natural home. They're the only part of the universe that we can experience directly and give us our unique perspective on life. How would you be here, reading this book, enjoying life, if it weren't for your body?

Our bodies are part of nature. They're made of the same natural elements found in trees, rocks, flowers, and other animals, and they connect us to the world through our senses. When our species first evolved, this sensory awareness was critical for survival. Seeing enabled us to find food, hearing helped us to be aware of predators, and touching gave us the ability to make fires and use tools. Our senses were also invaluable for forging social relationships, for example, through the use of language. This means that our senses are evolved and adapted to take in natural sights, sounds, and sensations.

Losing Touch with Our Senses

The problem is that in our modern lives, we've forgotten how to use them. This is hardly surprising when so many of us have jobs where we sit at desks, using merely fingertips and eyes. Moreover, we hardly spend any time outdoors. A recent survey by the UK's National Trust found that, on average, children now play outside each week for half the time their parents did when they were children. According to research by the Harvard School of Public Health, American adults spend less time outdoors than they do inside vehicles—less than five per cent

◆

I go to nature to be soothed and healed,

and to have my senses put in order.

JOHN BURROUGHS (1837–1921)
AMERICAN NATURALIST AND NATURE ESSAYIST

◆

of their day. As a result, our senses are rarely in touch with the natural world they evolved to live in. Instead, we spend our time in sterile, indoor settings cut off from natural changes in sights, sounds, and temperature. The sensory input we *do* receive tends to involve a continuous overload of images, sounds, and words, which we can struggle to process. This sensory overload can cause us stress, and it also feeds our addiction to constant stimulation and distraction. This means we've become significantly less mindful of what our senses have to tell us about the world in each moment. How can we pay them the attention they deserve if we're constantly shifting our attention from one thing to the next?

Our decreasing connection with our bodies and senses is having serious consequences for our well-being, resulting in conditions such as obesity, diabetes, depression, and anxiety. This isn't surprising if we're evolutionarily wired to spend time in nature. There's an urgent need for us to revitalize our bodies and senses—and mindful bird watching in open country and forests is a wonderful way to do this. So not only is bird watching pleasurable, but it is also good for us.

Bird Watching Is Good for Us

Why is spending time with our winged relatives so conducive to well-being? Above all, it encourages us out into the great outdoors while ensuring we pay attention to what we can see and hear. There's plenty of evidence that spending time in nature makes us healthier, less stressed, more creative, and happier. Patients in hospital rooms with natural views recover more rapidly from illness. Spending time outdoors reduces the symptoms of anxiety and depression. Studies of so-called "forest bathing" in Japan showed that mindful walks through forests reduced blood pressure and heart rate as well as levels of the stress hormone cortisol and activity of the sympathetic nervous system, with participants reporting better moods and lower anxiety after their forest walks. Spending time in nature captures our direct sensory experience, taking us out of our worried, overactive minds and into the present moment of our lives.

There's evidence that listening to birdsong, in particular, is good for our well-being. The beautiful tunes of our feathered performers not only relax our bodies but also enhance our concentration by stimulating our cognition. They take us into what's sometimes referred to as a state of "relaxed alertness." Why? Because for our ancestors, birdsong was the music of safety. If birds stopped singing, or sounded alarm calls, it was time to be on the lookout for predators. Birdsong is also nature's alarm clock, with the dawn chorus signaling the

beginning of a new day. This means that listening to birdsong can leave us feeling refreshed and relaxed, yet alert. The sounds of birdsong have also been shown to have therapeutic effects, helping patients recover from operations in hospitals with less pain and feeling more rested. For those of us experiencing low moods, there's evidence that listening to birdsong every day can help us to stay in good spirits.

In essence, bird watching is good for us because it requires us to be mindful and ensures that we invite fun, wonder, and beauty into our daily lives.

SENSORY CELEBRATIONS

◆

Birds have evolved a breathtaking array of songs, colors, shapes and flight patterns, and bird watching is a true sensory celebration of life. To witness this incredible diversity for ourselves, we simply need to open up our senses and walk with awareness.

On ONE MEMORABLE COUNTRYSIDE WALK last spring, I was struck by this magnificent variety. The sun was up, the sky was a brilliant blue, and the air was warm yet fresh. I was walking through what felt like an enchanted woodland. Standing alone among the trees, I stared at the bright green leaves as they danced in the sunlight and shadows, cradled by the breeze. They drew me into a peaceful trance from which I was gently awoken by the familiar melody

MINDFULNESS EXERCISE

THE BODY SCAN

An effective way to nurture body awareness is to practice an exercise called the body scan. The body, like the breath, is always with us. It's our day-to-day anchor for the practice of mindfulness, because our bodies exist only in the present moment. Moreover, body awareness is essential to mindful bird watching. How will we notice birds if we're lost in thoughts about the past and future? The more you practice the body scan, the more grounded and mindful of your senses you'll be, and the more marvels of the avian world you'll encounter.

Lie down with your arms by your side, palms facing up. Make sure you're comfortable. Become aware of how your body feels. Take a few slow, deep breaths and notice any resulting sensations. There's no right or wrong thing to experience.

Bring your attention to your feet. How do they feel? Are they cold or warm? Relaxed or tense? Or do you feel nothing in particular? That's fine, too.

One by one, bring all the other parts of your body into your awareness, and similarly notice any sensations in them. Are they pleasurable, painful, or neutral?

Whatever you experience, don't seek to change it or judge it. If thoughts come to mind, acknowledge them and gently return to the sensations in your body.

of a robin—the perfect musical overture for a gorgeous spring morning. I couldn't see him at first, but his bright red breast eventually caught my eye, perched among the flickering shadows and dappled light. Although his song was addressed to female robins in the neighborhood, I wanted to thank him for what felt like a personal welcome to his home.

Farther along the path, I stopped at a pond, sat down, and tuned in to the sounds of the robin's hidden world. I heard the

---

MINDFULNESS EXERCISE

THROUGH AN ARTIST'S EYES

Imagine yourself as an artist. Pretend that you're encountering what you're seeing for the first time and that you'd like to paint it. What would you need to know? You can practice mindful seeing with anything on view. If your mind wanders during the exercise, gently bring it back to what you're observing. Let's focus on birds, beginning with their shapes and colors. What shapes are their bodies and their beaks? What colors can you see on their feathers? Do the colors change in different lights? Do you notice any sheens, iridescence, or textures? How does their shape and color contrast with their surroundings? Next, consider their movements. Notice their gaits. Bring your awareness to their flight patterns. Do they soar, glide, or flap? Are they high up or low down? Do they fly alone or in flocks? Do they fly in a straight line or change direction? Discard common sense—lose yourself in the sensory experience.

initial slow and clear "chip-chip-chip" of a chaffinch proudly building up speed into a flourishing crescendo. Then came the remarkably loud, high-pitched wren shamelessly flaunting his virtuoso trilling, the humble whistled "see-saw" song of a chiffchaff and the confident "tee-cher, tee-cher" of the great tits. Then I heard one of my favorites: the accomplished, fluty warbling of a blackcap.

Seeing these songsters among the trees was surprisingly challenging. As I scanned the branches to find them, my frustrated eyes were unexpectedly compensated by a dazzle of electric blue darting across the pond. The kingfisher stole the sensory show as it perched on a branch overhanging the water: white flashes, russet, and mixed shades of blue, sprinkled with fluorescent stars. Simply stunning. After a few seconds it flew off, but the woodland symphony continued, leaving me little time to dwell on its departure.

I followed the path out of the woodland into a landscape of reed beds. Here, the soundtrack to my walk completely changed; a fabulous chorus of reed warblers echoed around me. Their repetitive, rasping, squeaky "churring" made me smile, reminding me of the robot R2-D2 from *Star Wars*. As I strained to see any telltale movements in the reeds that might have given away where they were hiding, my eyes were drawn to yet another sensory spectacle, quite possibly the climax of the morning. First one—then two, three, four, and finally five hobby falcons were soaring effortlessly overhead.

The agile flight of these slender birds was unbelievably powerful, with deep wingbeats followed by graceful arcing glides. I watched them through binoculars as they acrobatically caught dragonflies in their talons, lifting them to feed with impressive skill while still on the wing. As I gazed up at them against the azure sky, listening to the rustling reeds and feeling the warm sun on my face, I found myself momentarily immersed in an entrancing, mesmerizing flow of movement, color, and sound. My mind was quiet and my senses were invigorated—it felt wonderful to be alive.

Shapes, Colors & Movement
We can learn to tune into our senses one at a time, starting with our vision. We're rarely mindful of what we can see. This is in part because we rely so prominently on sight to take in the information we need for making practical decisions in our everyday lives. This means that we hardly ever take the time to appreciate and be curious about what we see. Farthermore, because of our use of language, we have a tendency to perceive the world as a set of separate objects—labelling them as tree, bird, cat, house—before moving on. What if we saw life—and birds, in particular—with a fresh, more mindful perspective?

The variety of colors and shapes exhibited by birds is tremendous. I've seen glorious painted buntings in Mexico with their stout beaks, bright blue heads, red chests, and

TAKE A SNAPSHOT

Take a walk with your camera and take photographs of the birds you come across. Zooming in on pictures of birds you've taken can be a great way to get a new, intimate perspective on the beauty to be found in the colors and patterns of birds' plumages. Their intricacy, vibrancy, and radiance will be sure to astonish you.

green, yellow, and gray backs. I've watched characterful todies in Cuban rain forests, with striking blue eyes, dazzling red throats, powder-blue collars, and fluorescent green heads. I've marveled at the ornate russet and black plumage of great crested grebes in lakes and wetlands.

However, one of my most precious encounters yet was with a bird species I encounter regularly at home. I was out walking locally one evening when I came across a solitary starling perched on top of a wooden post, lit by the late evening sun. Starlings are often regarded as common black birds and rarely receive much attention. But as I watched this one through my binoculars, I was struck by its astounding beauty. How could such a fantastic bird be so easily dismissed? Its black, white, and brown streaked feathers were covered in a glossy sheen of oily purples, yellows, and greens, all reflecting the golden light. No one else was around. It was just the starling and me—in a special moment—united by the soothing sound of the warm breeze.

The array of movements displayed by the avian world is equally fascinating. How do birds get around? Blackbirds and song thrushes hop, wagtails and crows walk, ducks waddle, and swans glide elegantly across still waters. You may notice the twirling of swifts high in summer skies, the undulating, bouncing flight of a woodpecker, the delicate hovering of a kestrel, the fast, zigzagging flight of a snipe, or the perfect V formation of geese on migration. I particularly enjoy watching barn owls hunting at dusk. Almost like an apparition, these silent, ghostlike hunters are incredibly graceful, flying low on buoyant wingbeats, back and forth across open fields and meadows. Birds are true masters of the air; follow them with your gaze and lose yourself in their dances through the skies.

The Soundtrack of Nature

When it comes to birdsong, there's nothing that can ever prepare you for the arresting experience of a spring dawn chorus. The transition between night and dawn in woodlands around the world is almost imperceptible to the eye, but not so to the ear. In my local woodland, the first song thrush breaks the night's silent stillness. It sings alone for a few minutes—clear, pure, loud musical phrases, each repeated a few times before moving on to the next. The luxury of being able to focus on the song of one eager individual belting out his morning solo is short-lived as other song thrushes join in. Soon, they're accompanied by fluting blackbirds, singing robins, trilling wrens,

warbling blackcaps, and flourishing chaffinches—rising to a competitive crescendo, a cacophony resonating across the woodland. It becomes almost impossible to tease apart individual performances. This acoustic and other similar worldwide extravaganzas are without a doubt one of the most transfixing experiences of spring.

Getting out in the early morning to experience the spring dawn chorus is a vital stop on your mindful bird-watching journey—you won't be disappointed. However, you don't need to get up at four o'clock to enjoy the music of the avian world. Although birds are most active at dawn and dusk, you'll hear them at almost any other time of day or year. Revel in the exhilaration of the Sprague's pipit's solo song while a skylark is suspended in the sky above you. Smile at the high-pitched notes

TUNING IN

Mindful listening is experiencing the sounds around us—taking the focus away from labelling what we hear, while bringing our awareness to the features of the sound itself. When you first listen to birds, all species may sound alike, but as you learn to tune in, you'll begin to notice differences. Is the song high-pitched or low-pitched? Does it sound fluid or scratchy? Can you pick up any repeated phrases or melodies? What differences do you notice between songs and calls? Do you notice differences between individuals? Close your eyes and be present with the sounds. If your mind wanders or seeks to label, gently bring it back to the sounds you can hear.

proudly broadcasted by the American redstart. Enjoy the laughing yaffle of the green woodpecker in the distance. Birds are our soundtrack to life. We need to experience it.

How Do They Make You Feel?

As you watch birds in open country and forests, notice how they make you feel. Do they energize you? Comfort you? Frustrate you? Calm you? Do they evoke memories? Simply become aware of what you experience. The courtship display flight of a pigeon uplifts me as it climbs skyward and then free falls into a glide. I find the rushed swooping of swallows over country streams and fields intensely exciting. The gentle drifting of waterbirds on still waters brings me calm and peace, and glimpsing a robin's red breast through the understory fills me with childlike joy every time. Experiencing birds with our

PRACTICE WITH OTHERS

Mindful seeing and listening can be a lot of fun to practice with others. Our experiences of the world can be infinitely diverse, so why not share our different perceptions of what's around us? Take a mindful bird-watching wander with friends or family. Spend a section of your walk in silence—and set yourselves the intention of bringing your awareness to any birds you see and hear. Then stop to discuss what you noticed and experienced. You'll be surprised at how much your experiences will vary!

senses can be thoroughly restorative and invigorating, whether we want to get away from life's everyday challenges or simply celebrate the glory of being alive.

In Sensory Harmony

One of the most awesome bird-watching experiences I have ever had was while watching the formation of a starling murmuration. When birds come together in flocks, the power of our sensory experience of them can be truly breathtaking. This wildlife spectacle occurs in fall at twilight around agricultural land, woodland, reed beds, cliffs, or buildings. One of the great things about starling murmurations is that we don't actually know how or why starlings engage in this extraordinary behavior. I delight in unexplained mysteries such as these, because they leave us with only the pure wonder of our direct experience.

I was taking an evening walk through a local nature reserve and toward the end of my stroll groups of starlings began to gather, forming small flocks over the fields in the distance. Over the following fifteen minutes, the separate flocks united into an enormous swarm of thousands of birds, which began to perform a mesmerizing aerial ballet, whirling and diving through the sky. This massive "super being" shape-shifted into unpredictable formations as the birds twisted and turned through the air. I will never forget the thrilling moment when the flock flew straight over my head. I was both enchanted by

the quiet fluttering of thousands of beating wings and over-whelmed by the power of this astonishing winged mass. How could each individual starling find exactly the right position among its neighbors to form this incredible super being, turning in perfect unison? Being in absolute harmony with the flock must have required a profound awareness of their surroundings—and the starlings were thus a true inspiration to be present with our senses. The connectedness of birds with the world around them is one of the reasons they're excellent messengers of what is happening in our natural world.

EAVESDROPPING ON AVIAN CONVERSATIONS

Listen to birds. They have a lot to tell us about the natural world—if we pay attention. Tuning into bird language immediately reveals the interconnectedness of all life and offers us invaluable insights into developing a wiser relationship with nature.

DUE TO OUR INNATE CONNECTION with nature, mindful bird watching is undoubtedly a tonic and a source of peace for our modern hearts and minds. For our ancestors, however, having an in-depth awareness and understanding of birds and nature was vital. For this reason, they were acutely tuned into their senses and natural instincts. They paid close attention to what they could see, hear, and smell, because their survival depended on it.

A deep awareness and understanding of birdcalls, bird-songs and behaviors became an integral part of our ancestors' daily lives. Birds informed them of the happenings in the wilderness. This appreciation of what is often called "bird language" is still part of the culture of many native communities, such as the San Bushmen of the Kalahari Desert and some Amazon rainforest communities. In our modern lives, however, most of us don't *need* to read the language of our winged companions to survive, but we can still gain great pleasure and insights from tuning into their conversations.

What is Bird Language?

Bird language is their expression of what they're experiencing. Have you ever seen a robin lifting its tail up and down when he becomes threatened and agitated, because of a competing male invading his territory? Or perhaps delighted at the sight of a relaxed wood thrush broadcasting his spring tune from the treetops with confident exaltation?

Put simply, birds talk. They discuss everything and everyone. They talk to each other. They talk to potential and existing partners. They discuss territories, predators, and other animals, using a combination of calls, songs, and body language. Bird language is the communication within and between species that birds use to stay in contact with a flock, find partners, protect their territories, and stay aware while they go about their daily business.

A pair of song sparrows will emit short "companion calls" to check they're both still nearby and out of danger. Great tits will inform their flock that an owl or sparrow hawk is nearby or hunting overhead by alarm calling. While in Mexico, I once witnessed a mixed-species flock of tanagers, flycatchers, hummingbirds, and warblers calling loudly as a large snake moved through the leaf litter below them. Bird language isn't only of value to the birds themselves but also to other creatures, such as deer and rabbits, which listen out for bird alarm calls as an early warning of potential danger. The language of birds has been extensively studied by the lifelong birder, tracker, and naturalist Jon Young, one of the leaders in understanding animal communication.

Why Understand Bird Language?

Understanding bird language is above all a continuation of our mindful bird-watching journey, because it requires mindful listening and mindful seeing so that we can pick up on the differences between birdcalls, birdsongs and behaviors. But tuning into bird language is also a way for us to discover what's happening around us when we're out in nature, such as whether other animals are present. In response to an owl sleeping against a tree trunk or a deer walking by, birds modify their behaviors and vocalizations. As we detect these changes in bird activity, we can discover what other creatures may be in the vicinity. In this light, a better understanding of

bird language can enable us to experience more encounters with wildlife, including birds.

People who have studied bird language also report that it can enhance aspects of their modern lives—including their perception of human relationships, their creativity, and their sense of interdependence with the world. At a time when we urgently need to restore our connection with our sensory experience and with the natural world around us, understanding bird language is beneficial to us all. It can help us nurture a wiser relationship with nature. No expertise is required—simply mindful awareness and experience. Start by finding yourself a "Sit Spot."

The Sit Spot

My grandad used to tell me that if you want to get up close and personal with birds, you must sit and remain still for at least twenty minutes. After that time, the birds you spooked on your arrival into their personal space would begin to relax and return. I later discovered the Sit Spot exercise on a nature-awareness course I attended, and my grandad, like so many times before, turned out to be right.

The Sit Spot is a wonderful exercise you can practice regularly to enhance your experience when you're in nature—paying full attention to your senses, watching and listening to birds around you. In this case, the best place to sit may be in the heart of a forest, by a stream, or somewhere with a

MINDFULNESS EXERCISE

SIT SPOT

The Sit Spot is a wonderful way to train your senses in nature—and a place from which you can tune into bird language. Visit your Sit Spot daily, ideally for twenty to forty minutes. Sit or lie down, and be still and quiet once you're there. As you sit, simply notice what you can see, hear, smell, touch. Take a journal to make notes.

Getting there

Before heading to your Sit Spot, take a deep breath. Set an intention to let go of any other concerns and engage your senses.

Don't hunt. Let your senses drift across the landscape. Walk without a goal. You aren't trying to see things. You're simply opening up your awareness. Keep your head up and try not to lean forward. Take shorter steps. Glide quietly and look at everything.

In your Sit Spot

- *Watch mindfully* Pick a point of focus ahead. Notice what you see. While staring at that point, notice what you see in your peripheral vision. Turn your head, pick another point of focus ahead, and reengage your peripheral vision.
- *Listen mindfully* Notice sounds. Notice the silence between sounds. Listen to the farthest sounds you can hear around you.
- *Touch mindfully* Notice what you can feel. Is the ground cold? What can you feel on your skin?
- *Participate* Notice how you're feeling—what energy are you bringing to the place? Cultivate an attitude of belonging and participation, instead of being merely an observer.
- *Practice!*

natural view devoid of obvious signs of human presence. You can do this wherever you are. As your senses get more and more accustomed to the natural world, you will begin to discover things you'd never noticed before.

You can also use the Sit Spot to deepen your understanding of bird language and what it tells you about in a specific location. The more present you are with all your senses, the more tuned in to bird language you will become. Here, the most important criterion for your Sit Spot location is that you pick somewhere close to where you live, so that you can get there every day, even if this is in your yard. The more you visit your Sit Spot, the more familiar you'll become with its visitors and their behaviors day by day, season after season. Gradually, you will learn to tune into "radio bird."

Tuning Into Radio Bird

Listening to birds is like listening to nature's radio. They'll give you the news updates, from the weather to the traffic to what's happening in the area. They're great news readers because they're the animals that react most visibly and audibly to what's going on. Moreover, birds don't fly, sing, or call for no reason. They must save their energy to survive. Therefore, when you notice birds singing, calling, or flying off, ask yourself why they may be doing so.

The secret to understanding bird language lies within us—in curiosity and practice. Pay a daily visit to your Sit Spot.

Become familiar with it. Get to know the birds there. Tune in to their calls and watch their behaviors and notice how they change. After twenty minutes of sitting, birdcalls will change from initial repetitive, loud alarm calls to songs and companion calls as they start to feed again. Birds are always commenting on the degree of harmony or stress around them. In time, you'll become more familiar with various vocalizations and their meanings.

BIRD VOCALIZATIONS

Understanding bird language takes a lot of patience and practice. Here are some of the main types of vocalization to listen out for:

- *Songs* Long, melodious mixes of sounds—usually heard in spring when birds are attracting partners and setting up territories. They don't sing when anxious, so if you hear birdsong, it's unlikely there will be predators nearby.
- *Companion calls* Gentle, repetitive sounds that birds use all year round to keep track of each other while feeding. Companion calls are a sign the birds feel safe and probably mean there are no nearby predators.
- *Territorial aggression* Loud calling, and wing flapping, between two birds. This is an argument about territorial boundaries.
- *Alarm calls* Often a louder version of companion calls, but when an aerial predator is around you might hear a thin, high-pitched sound. Birds have different alarm calls for different predators. The more you investigate the sources of alarms, the more you'll learn to recognize some of them.

Understanding bird language also enables us to develop a deeper understanding of our own impact on birds and the rest of nature around us. Our state of mind and our attitude have a strong impact on nature and wildlife around us.

WALKING WITH ATTITUDE

Birds are so sensitive to the world's sights and sounds that they can even sense our body language. This means that our attitude when bird watching really matters. It impacts the birds themselves, but it also affects our own bird-watching experience.

THE FACT THAT BIRDS CAN SENSE our attitude seems almost unbelievable, but last fall I experienced it first-hand on the nature-awareness course I attended. I took a daily walk through a nearby forest most mornings and experimented with different walking attitudes to observe how the birds responded. I quickly discovered that if I strode through the forest head down, paying little attention to the birds, they began their loud alarm calling. Next, I tried creeping up on a chaffinch I had heard singing in the trees above me. I tried to hide from it to avoid it seeing me and searched for it intently through my binoculars. To my surprise, it began alarm calling. Was I making too much noise? Had it seen me?

When I explained this to the course leader he said: "You're in hunting mode, you've entered his territory. You can't fool

If we learn to read the birds—and their
behaviors and vocalizations—through them,
we can read the world at large … if we replace
collision with connection, learn to read these details,
feel at home, relax, and are respectful—ultimately
the birds will yield to us the first rite of passage:
a close encounter with an animal otherwise
wary of our presence.

FROM "WHAT THE ROBIN KNOWS:
HOW BIRDS REVEAL THE SECRETS OF THE NATURAL WORLD"
JON YOUNG

---

him, he knows." He suggested an alternative approach: "Walk with awareness, be mindful of sights and sounds around you. Don't seek them out or pursue them. Just be open and aware." I was astonished by the result. This time, when I heard a chaffinch singing in the tree, I moved away from it and walked around it. The chaffinch stopped singing and flew to a higher branch, but he didn't alarm call. He found a comfortable distance to sit and watch me from. He definitely knew I was there, like I knew he was. He was probably a little nervous at first, but I was respecting his territory and personal space and we weren't presenting a threat to each other. After a few moments, he appeared to relax and burst into song—what a beautiful, unique moment of understanding with the wild.

A Respect for Birds & Nature

Our attitude in nature matters—let us be mindful of our impact on birds' lives. The way we are in nature is important above all because birds are sentient beings. They have an inherent right to live their lives and deserve our deepest respect. Through compassion, we can learn to reduce the disturbance we cause them as we visit the forests, woodlands, rivers, and lakes they call home. Life in the wild can be tough and we must strive to support birds to live the lives they have evolved to live, wherever we possibly can.

Farthermore, the attitude we carry when bird watching also affects our own experience of watching birds. As we come to our senses—receptive, quiet, and mindful—we can begin to blend in with the natural world around us, becoming part of the sacred silence of the wild. Through our growing understanding of bird language, we can start to build trust with our winged relatives. This trust can increase the quality and quantity of our shared moments with them. The greater respect we show our avian companions, the more likely they'll be to gift us with their extraordinary beauty.

◆

In order to see birds,

you have to become part of the silence.

ROBERT WILSON LYND (1879–1949)
IRISH WRITER AND ESSAYIST

◆

CHAPTER THREE

DANCING WITH WAVES

Bird watching by the sea is the ideal inspiration for learning to let go of our mind's narratives. The more we let go, the more happiness we welcome into our lives and the greater pleasure we gain from our moments with birds. In energetic coastal environments, we find ourselves amid the elements— surrounded by rocks, waves, and wind. As birds effortlessly blend into this landscape of freedom, we give in to the flow of life, drawn to the present of each fleeting moment.

I felt an intense sense of liberation as I stood
barefoot on the beach that afternoon. My feet were buried
in the sand; I felt strong and steady as I leaned into the wind.
It had been a stressful week—and it was such a beautiful relief to
be on the coast. I watched the gulls as they rode the air currents
up and down the beach. I contemplated a common tern as it drifted,
elegantly buoyant, over tall waves. Small flocks of sanderlings were
racing around on the shore like clockwork toys. In the distance,
a cormorant launched clumsily from the sea's surface. As I watched
the birds, the crashing waves broke down my worries and washed
them out to sea. The unpredictable dynamism of this vast open
space between the horizon and me helped disperse the week's
challenges. It was as if the birds, the wind, and the sea were
helping me to loosen my grip on them. The week's stresses no
longer mattered; like the shells being dropped by the
gulls farther along the beach in their attempts
to crack them open, I was free to let them go.

THE CALL OF FREEDOM

❖

As human beings, we can sometimes feel trapped—by our upbringing, social norms, or judgments—preventing us from living authentically. As we learn to let go, mindfulness enables us to restore our freedom to experience ourselves as we truly are.

HAVE YOU EVER HAD THE FEELING that you want to set yourself free but simultaneously feel afraid? It may be that you're dying to get on the dance floor at a party but are scared of what others may think. Or that you want to stop dwelling on a breakup but are addicted to the thought of your lost love. Or perhaps you want to apply for a new job but fear the unknown. We all experience this yearning for freedom, while at the same time fearing the changes it may bring. This inner struggle can be distressing, but rest assured, you're not alone. It's one of the wonderful contradictions we all experience as conscious human beings.

Just as birds have the courage to let go of the branch they're perched on in order to fly, we, too, can let go of

❖

Letting go gives us freedom

and freedom is the only condition for happiness.

THICH NHAT HANH (1926–2022)
VIETNAMESE BUDDHIST MONK AND PEACE ACTIVIST

❖

our own "branches." We hold onto beliefs, memories, posses-sions, and identity, because we fear the unknown. By letting go, birds are able to enjoy their lives from a myriad of other vantage points. What if we learned to let go—allowing our-selves to live wholeheartedly? Letting go isn't easy—so what is it that prevents us from soaring freely through life? What do we need to let go of? The answers are found in our relation-ship with our beautiful, fascinating conscious minds.

The Grips of the Mind

The mind has been defined in many different ways in different cultures, religions, and belief systems. Some believe it's some-thing that only humans possess, whereas others—including animist traditions, such as Hinduism and some Native Ameri-can cultures—believe that the mind is a spiritual essence found in all natural things, whether they're animals, plants, rocks, or people. Although cognitive science is progressing fast, we still don't understand fully how the human mind works or how consciousness is made possible. However, what we do have is a direct experience of our minds on a daily basis.

The mind is a superb instrument if used rightly.

Used wrongly, however, it becomes very destructive.

FROM "THE POWER OF NOW: A GUIDE TO SPIRITUAL ENLIGHTENMENT"
ECKHART TOLLE

What is the Mind?

Close your eyes. Notice any thoughts. Are they pleasant, unpleasant, or neutral? Become aware of how you're feeling. Are you happy? Sad? Indifferent? Relaxed? Stressed? These experiences are what we commonly refer to as the "mind"—home to our thoughts and emotions. Thanks to our conscious minds, we've developed the ability to communicate through language, created endless beauty through art, and gained an in-depth understanding of awe-inspiring phenomena through science. However, left unchecked, our minds can remove us from the present, direct experience of our lives.

MINDFULNESS EXERCISE

THE STORYTELLER

Sit upright, relaxed yet alert. Notice your breath, bringing your awareness to its sensations. Now bring your attention to any thoughts. Don't pursue them or push them away. Simply observe them, welcoming them with kindness. Label them as "plan," "worry," "memory," and so on, and then let them go. Notice your mind's constant storytelling throughout the day. What are its favorite narratives? What habits has it developed? How do they make you feel? Notice how the stories come and go and constantly change. Let them arise, be there, and pass. Remember to be kind toward yourself as you do so.

Directing Our Precious Attention

Have you ever caught yourself walking to a store but being unaware of what's around you? Or perhaps found yourself day-dreaming while socializing with friends? We can often find ourselves unknowingly captivated by our mind's constant commentaries—its worries, plans, cravings, and judgments. This is known as being on autopilot. In this mode, our awareness drifts and we take no active role in directing its focus. Instead, we let our mind do the job, letting it take control and absorb our attention—taking us away from the here and now.

Why does this matter? People often ask: "What if I don't always want to live in the present? What if I like to daydream and make plans?" But these questions are based on a common misconception. Mindfulness isn't giving up on conscious thought. It doesn't mean we stop thinking. Instead, it's developing a gentle awareness of our experience in each moment, including our thoughts and emotions, so that we can make

OUR EMOTIONAL LIFE

Become familiar with your emotions. Notice any bodily sensations that accompany them. Notice where you feel them and let them be as they are. Try to show an interest in them, whether they're pleasurable, painful, or neutral. Don't seek to get rid of them. Welcome them when they arise and then let them go. Our emotions bring us to life.

wise choices about what we pay attention to. By wise choices, I mean those that increase long-term happiness and well-being while decreasing suffering—for ourselves and others.

A Matter of Choice

If you're on the train daydreaming about your next vacation, you may choose to indulge those thoughts. But if you're in a meeting with your boss, it may not be wise to. Moreover, when we're entertaining thoughts of anger, blame, or self-criticism, living on autopilot can leave us unwittingly giving in to the tyranny of these narratives. This is distressing at the time, but can also lead us to act in ways that cause farther suffering to ourselves and others. Listening to blaming thoughts toward a friend who inadvertently upset you may cause you to get unjustifiably angry with them, perpetuating tension in your friendship. Giving in to thoughts of inadequacy when not reaching the end of your to-do list may result in you pushing yourself to get everything done—and never taking a break. This is particularly relevant to our fast-paced modern lives; there'll always be another email to respond to. But is this constant busyness conducive to sustainable well-being? For most of us, it isn't. Why not take a proactive role in what we pay attention to and how we act instead of letting our mind run the show? What if we freed ourselves from our mind's apparent grip over the course of our life?

Nurturing a wise relationship with our mind is the journey of a lifetime, but the first step is to get to know it like you would a friend—with kindness and acceptance. Notice its favorite stories. Be curious about how it responds to events in your life. Be compassionate toward yourself as you do this; our minds aren't always easy companions. In time, we recognize that our minds aren't messengers of the truth; thoughts are merely constantly changing stories and emotions are transient. Observe them. Watch them come and go like gulls soaring up and down the beach over the waves.

How we respond to the content of our mind is paramount when it comes to our well-being. We have the power to decide where we direct our precious attention and how to act as a consequence. Mindfulness is the awareness that gives us this power; if we're aware of what's going on in our mind, the choice is ours in each moment.

SURFING THE WAVES OF THE MIND

Imagine you're swimming in the ocean. The waves are your thoughts and emotions—they will take you where they please. Now imagine that you have a surfboard called Mindfulness. You stand on it and ride the waves. You still move around, rising and falling—but your destination is not being controlled by the sea anymore. Instead, the waves come and go—and you remain strong and steady. If you fall off, be kind toward yourself; don't worry, just hop back on!

THE MIND'S FAVORITE HABITS

◆

Shaped by our evolutionary past and personal experiences, our minds are creatures of habit, functioning using learned patterns and processes. Becoming familiar with these habits is the key to learning to let go—to discovering who we really are.

As we become more acquainted with our thoughts and emotions, we start to notice our mind's favorite habits. Do you analyze? Plan? Judge? What emotions do you experience the most? The narratives of our thinking minds are infinitely diverse—each of us experiencing a unique stream of consciousness. Nevertheless, a large proportion of our thought patterns revolve around our desire to feel in control—in charge of our day-to-day destiny. Why might this be?

The Controlling Mind

Our minds, like our bodies, evolved in the natural world. When we roamed the African savanna around 100,000 years ago, our ability to plan, analyze, and innovate enabled us to survive in a diversity of habitats. In an uncertain natural world, it was important for us to control our daily lives.

Our minds evolved to become excellent problem solvers and resource seekers; our lives depended on food, shelter, sexual partners, and social relationships. We became experts at controlling and changing our environments to ensure we

were always prepared, for example hoarding food for times of scarcity. Around 10,000 years ago, we gained even greater control over our resources through the development of agriculture. Later, towns and cities, as well as economic, religious, and political systems, became instrumental in maintaining order and control over a rapidly growing population.

Negativity Bias

The success of our species was enhanced by our minds' negativity bias; those who were fearful and prepared for a predator's attack would evade it and were more likely to survive than the individuals who weren't. In the interest of survival, nature shaped our minds to overestimate threats and underestimate opportunities and the availability of resources. This gave us more control to thrive amid the unpredictability of the wild. Put simply, our mind was built with a greater sensitivity to unpleasant news. Having brains that are wired to make us afraid, anxious, and alert was evolutionarily advantageous; it was an ideal way to escape life's natural dangers and enable us to procreate. However, now that survival is less of an immediate concern for most of us, our controlling minds can hinder the quality of modern life.

It's no surprise that our ability to control aspects of our external worlds has given us high hopes of controlling other parts of our existence. However, many aspects of our lives aren't within our control. We have no say over the weather or

the train being late. Moreover, we can't control our inner worlds; we can't rid ourselves of thoughts and emotions we don't want. If I said, "Don't think of a purple elephant!," what would come to mind? A purple elephant! If I said, "Try not to feel sad," would you feel happier? No, you'd probably just feel more frustrated that you were feeling low.

Our resource-seeking and threat-avoiding minds are wired to desire what we like and avoid what we don't. If we believe these narratives, we delude ourselves and think that we can control all aspects of our experience. Yet as we all know, life doesn't always go our way. Thinking and behaving as if it should can cause us a lot of unnecessary pain and frustration.

The Separating Mind

Our mind also likes to organize our experience of life into separate, labeled "boxes"—primarily through our use of language. This helps us break down a universe that may otherwise seem overwhelming. We separate and categorize what we take in with our senses into words—trees, roots, leaves, birds, songs, oceans. These labels help us understand and communicate about the world. But this separation is artificial; in reality, everything is interconnected and constantly changing. Nothing is fixed and substantial. What we call a tree is the part that we see, but a tree has roots underground to take in water and nutrients from the soil, and exchanges carbon dioxide for oxygen in the air. Trees can't live in isolation; they can only

exist in relation to the rest of nature. The same is true for all life. Here too, our mind's perception of the world goes against how things really are. A similar principle applies to how we perceive our "selves."

Who Are You?

If I asked you who you are, what would you say? Perhaps you're a physician, a lawyer, or an accountant? But if you changed job, that identity would disappear. You may then refer to your family, friends, or nationality. But that's who you are in relation to others, which may change throughout your life. Could we define you by your personality or what you value? Are you shy? Generous? Passionate about music? This is more about what motivates your actions. So who are you, independent of all this?

Try as we might, we'll never find a fixed, stable entity that we can pinpoint as our "selves." Instead, our experience of ourselves depends on an infinite number of constantly changing conditions affecting our habits, thoughts, and emotions. Our perceived "I" comes in and out of our awareness throughout the day and frequently changes its tune. One moment it tells you "I feel on top of the world," and the next "I'm a failure." In essence, we're metaphorically reborn in each moment, depending on what we're experiencing. Cognitive scientists have recently come to this same conclusion: There is no separate, fixed, independent entity that we can call our self.

Our Illusionary Ego

Our minds hold memories of our past experiences and visions of our future experiences alongside thinking patterns and behavioral habits that shape our personalities. This leaves us with the impression that our "I" is an independent entity going through life. But this perception is an illusion created by our minds. In essence, our selves are constantly changing interconnected processes—like the rest of the natural world.

Moreover, as we develop our mindfulness practice, we'll begin to notice how attached we are to our illusory fixed "self;" we call it our "ego." Our mind invests a lot of effort to protect our ego from potential threat through our likes and dislikes, views, judgments, and assumptions about ourselves and the rest of the world. We fear other people's opinions, we feel the need for our views and opinions to be right, requiring recognition and praise. These thoughts are part of being human and are perfectly normal—we all experience them. But if we give in to them, they can lead to egocentric behaviors, such as people pleasing, attention seeking,

---

◆

By letting it go it all gets done.

The world is won by those who let it go.

But when you try and try, the world is beyond winning.

LAO TZU (FL. SIXTH CENTURY BCE)
CHINESE PHILOSOPHER AND FOUNDER OF TAOISM

◆

aggressive words and actions, and perpetual striving to demonstrate our worth. These behaviors are rarely conducive to our happiness and well-being. And why invest so much energy in protecting an illusion?

Letting Go

Why are we so addicted to believing our mind's delusional stories? The primary reason is that we're afraid to let go of the familiar and move into the unknown, so we cling to our habitual patterns of thinking and being. Yet we crave aliveness and freedom, creating an internal tug-of-war. What if we ended our struggle to control the uncontrollable? We have the power to learn to let go in each moment.

LETTING GO

Letting go of the contents of our mind is loosening our grip on them, letting them come and go without getting entangled in them. Is your mind wishing that it would stop raining when you're caught in a thunderstorm? Is your mind criticizing you for something you did wrong? Or blaming you or someone else for how you are feeling today? Notice these thoughts. Thank your mind for doing its job of trying to keep you safe. Take note of any information that could lead to any useful, wise action. Then let it go, by coming back to your direct experience in the present moment—to your body and your breath. What is with you and around you right now? The more you practice, the more letting go will become natural to you.

Our minds are storytellers. Through awareness, we can let go of their unhelpful narratives. What if we stopped living in the realm of our mind and came back to our direct experience? Letting go isn't easy for any of us—our social norms condition us to be in control and conform our thoughts and behaviors to those around us. Identify what you can and can't control. Change what you can control and let everything else go. Letting go is a challenge—but birds can help us.

INSPIRED BY BIRDS TO LET GO

Haven't we all gazed at a bird soaring through the sky? Haven't we longed to experience the freedom our winged relatives have to break away from the grips of the earth? Watching birds is a wonderful inspiration for letting go. Coastal birds, in particular, are great messengers of freedom.

RECENTLY, I WAS WANDERING along a rocky beach before going on a coastal walk with friends, when my mind began to entertain self-critical thoughts about the chores I'd failed to complete. "Why are you at the seashore when you should be at home sorting out your paperwork?" Just as I became aware of the tyrannical narratives of my mind, I saw a common tern, flying back and forth along the shore. Common terns are elegant white and silver birds, sometimes known as "sea swallows" due to their long, forked tail streamers. I was

instantly captivated by its floating, weightless flight, high above the rolling waves. It drifted through the air, gracefully borrowing the wind with each wingbeat—leaning into it as its wings drifted down and letting it go as they glided back up. As it did so, it scanned the ocean looking for fish. In that moment, the tern inspired the awareness I needed to observe the rolling waves in my mind. I cradled my thoughts in my awareness, observing them and loosening my grip on them, like the tern lightly holding onto the wind from its high vantage point. The self-critical narratives in my mind faded as I let them go, and I brought my attention back to the beautiful bird flying out toward the horizon.

Absolute Presence

Although our mind's ability to visit the past and future can be extremely valuable, life can only be truly experienced in the present, where there are no worries and anxieties. As often as possible, practice noticing what takes you away from each moment and return to your direct experience of the here and now. When you notice yourself drifting off into your mind's stories, bring your awareness kindly back to your breath and body, and take in what's around you with your senses. Ask yourself, "What can I see, hear, and feel right now?" When we cease our addiction to living in regret of the past and hope for the future, and bring ourselves to the present, happiness and well-being effortlessly trickle into our lives.

I remember once watching a loud, cackling breeding colony of gannets. Hundreds of impressive, agile birds circled out to sea and back toward the dramatic white cliffs that plunged down into the water below me. I delighted in their pure white plumage with beautiful black-pointed wing tips, which looked like they had been dipped in ink. As I looked through my binoculars at individual birds sitting on the cliff side, I noticed the powder blue ring and striking black lining around their eyes. The tops of their heads were dusted in ocher and their long beaks were pointed like daggers.

As I became absorbed by their beauty, it felt effortless to let go of anything other than what was before my eyes and ears. My gaze followed one of the birds as it launched itself off the cliff into the air and glided out to sea on outspread wings. Majestic and free, it rode the wind with incredible ease. After flapping its way back to the cliff, it turned to face into the wind again. The stunning bird hung there, focused and responding to every movement of the air currents. The gusts of wind were powerful and unpredictable and any distraction may have caused it to lose its balance. The past and future had no place for this dazzling aerial acrobat—only now, only the next gust of wind mattered.

Although our mind's ability to visit the past and future can be valuable, life can only be truly experienced in the present.

◆

Knowledge is learning something new every day.
Wisdom is letting go of something every day.

ZEN PROVERB

◆

Going with the Flow

When we're faced with experiences we can't control, it's best
to let life take its course, accepting it as it comes. Our lives
undeniably involve both pleasure and pain; in fact, we can't
experience one without the other. Nevertheless, we don't
need to create more pain for ourselves by holding onto past
pleasure and striving to avoid present and future pain. We can
simply respond to life moment by moment, making the best
of what each day brings. Imagine you are a tern, drifting in
flight over a calm sea, noticing and experiencing the different
colors, shapes, and sounds around you as they pass by. Enjoy
it. Learn from it. Experience it.

Sanderlings on wave-washed beaches are a great inspiration for going with the flow. These tiny, plump, energetic
wading birds gather in loose flocks, running back and forth
over wet sand. They wait for the sea to retreat then begin
probing avidly for the mollusks and crustaceans they feed on.
Because these marine invertebrates leave no trace when they
burrow into the sand as the water moves away, the sanderlings
catch their food by plunging their beaks into the sand at

random, eating whatever they find. These charming gray, black, and white birds are comical to watch; their short black legs blur as they rapidly scuttle up and down the beach, responding to the ebb and flow of the waves. They're in harmony with the natural rhythms of the sea over which they have no control, mimicking the waves with their hurried dance. Perhaps we could all learn to dance a little more with the waves in our lives?

LETTING GO IN MINDFUL BIRD WATCHING

◆

In that special moment when we first meet a bird, our "beginner's mind" is captured—we're filled with curiosity, questions, and possibilities. But once our mind kicks in with its labels, knowledge, memories, and judgments, we're dragged out of our direct experience.

WHY DOES THIS MATTER? Because the more we know and remember, the shorter that fascinating instant of not knowing becomes. We reduce the precious space that contains the marvel and wonder there is to be found in our moments with birds. For some experts, it can almost disappear—remember my friend from chapter one, who had lost his appreciation of common birds? If we always watch birds in this way, with our minds instead of our hearts, we may start to close the door to their infinite beauty. However, through the practice of mindfulness, we can turn this around.

The moment the little boy is concerned
with which is a jay and which is a sparrow, he can
no longer see the birds or hear them sing.

FROM "GAMES PEOPLE PLAY"
ERIC BERNE (1910–1970)

It's the nurturing of this space known as "mindful awareness" that mindful bird watching is all about. Being comfortable with "not-knowing" is a challenge for our controlling mind. But we aren't giving up on naming, learning and categorizing. Knowledge and understanding are invaluable. Instead, mindful bird watching is an invitation to go beyond the narratives of our mind to relax into the beautiful mystery of our pure, untouched experience.

What's in a Name?

As we explored in chapter one, naming bird species is a great way to celebrate and understand the diversity of the natural world. Moreover, because learning requires discernment and discrimination, naming is functional. But as we grow our bird species identification skills, it's easy to get caught up in the act of naming as an end in itself—perhaps neglecting our enjoyment when bird watching. There have been many occasions when naming birds has sufficiently satisfied my mind, causing me to move on without fully appreciating them.

I recall one particular cloudy afternoon when I saw a small group of medium-size, brownish, wading birds impressively camouflaged on a rocky beach. My mind immediately recognized them as turnstones from their stocky shape, stout beaks and intermittent, obsessive pecking behavior. I had seen birds of this species before and, being in a bad mood, dwelling on an argument I had with a friend that morning, I didn't engage any farther and wandered on.

A few seconds later, I heard their endearing high-pitched staccato call behind me as I walked away. It was almost as if they were asking me to go beyond their name, give them a second chance, and gift them some attention. I gave into their wise attempt to call me back to the present moment, remembering that I had my binoculars in my backpack. I sat on a wall looking out to sea and took time to observe them. I noticed their striking tortoiseshell plumage. They were reddish brown with blackish-brown patches on the upperparts, and white on the underparts, with a black-and-white head,

---

Words can express no more than a tiny
fragment of human knowledge, for what we can
say and think is always immeasurably less than
what we experience.

FROM "THE WAY OF LIBERATION"
ALAN WATTS (1915–1973)

LETTING GO IN BIRD WATCHING

If your mind interrupts with a name or knowledge while you're watching a bird, acknowledge it. Thank your mind for the information, but remind yourself that your intention is to be present with the bird, to really experience its qualities with awareness—beyond information or labels. Come back to what you see and hear in that moment—focus on all shapes, colors, movements, sounds and behaviors—while letting go of your mind's intervention. Repeat this as often as you need to. You can always come back to finding out more about the species name or ecology later on.

throat, neck, and breast. The markings of each bird were slightly different; no two were identical. I then delighted in watching one of them use its strong neck and upturned bill to bulldoze an impressively large stone. I hoped it had found a worthwhile, delicious mollusk underneath to reward that effort! It had incredible force for a creature so small—and the power to uplift my mood. I smiled as its species name—turnstone—suddenly gained renewed meaning.

Our mind likes naming things because of its addiction to separation. It learns to home in on a few recognizable shapes, colors, and sounds, which enables it to categorize birds quickly. In time, we can easily fall into a pattern of notice, label, and move on. The more we do this, the more we close up that special space where mindful awareness allows for

wonder and appreciation to blossom. Notice your mind's ability to name, hold the name in your awareness, and then gently let it go. Go beyond the name, beyond your thinking mind, and into your experience—right now.

Keeping an Open Mind

Einstein was a regular mindfulness practitioner. When asked why he was successful in his field, he often said it was almost entirely due to keeping in touch with his childlike wonder about the world. Although he had tremendous scientific knowledge, he was occasionally willing to let go of what he knew and ask questions a child would ask. Indeed, if we hold on too tightly to acquired knowledge, we can become jaded and hinder our creativity. True innovation and discovery only arise if we look at the world with a beginner's mind, letting go of preconceptions about what we may or may not encounter.

One of my friends who hadn't spent much time watching birds once went on an organized group nature walk in a coastal reserve. Many people in the group were regular visitors to the reserve, so she was looking forward to learning about the birds they came across.

I know one thing, that I know nothing.

SOCRATES (471–399 BCE)
GREEK PHILOSOPHER

As they walked out toward the sea across coastal marshes, they passed a large gathering of spoonbills. Spoonbills are white, heron-shaped birds with fantastic black bills like spatulas. They're often seen asleep, bills tucked firmly into their backs. The group took a quick glance at the birds but most had seen sleepy spoonbills here before and walked on. My friend, however, stopped to observe these incredible creatures, having never seen them before. She asked one of the group members, "Are there babies at the back?" With great confidence came the immediate reply: "No, spoonbills don't breed here. They haven't bred in the UK for 300 years and only started breeding in the country again a few years ago. It'll be a while before we see baby spoonbills here!" My friend humbly assumed the regular visitor would know best.

On their way back that afternoon, the group walked past the spoonbills once more. Another group member stopped and observed them again. Suddenly, he exclaimed, "Young ones!" As the others excitedly crowded around him with their binoculars, they saw seven spoonbill chicks with their short, pink "spoon bills," begging for food from their parents. A beautiful, intimate sight that hadn't been seen there for more than 300 years—and my friend had seen them earlier.

The world isn't always as predictable as we'd like to believe. If we're willing to see it, there's always something new to discover. Farthermore, knowledge can lead us to hold expectations that, when unmet, cause disillusion. See if you

can occasionally let go of knowledge and common sense—go with the flow and enjoy whatever you find. Birds don't turn up on demand, so why not let go of our expectations that they should? Explore with an open mind; you never know what marvels you may encounter on your way. Great minds expect nothing while considering all possibilities, no matter how outrageous they may appear.

Letting Yourself Go

Why do we hold on to names, knowledge, and expectations so tightly? Ultimately, the answer is in our relationship with our ego. We become attached to our perceived identity as a knowledgeable birder, an expert botanist or an experienced historian. To not name or know is to give up the self that prides itself on this knowledge.

Mindfulness takes us beyond ordinary thinking into a wordless awareness that unites us with what we see, hear, smell, touch, and taste. This is where life's vitality lies. In the space of not-knowing, we are free from our mind's control, united with the world around us as the separation between us and the world begins to fade. This is the ultimate freedom where, in the present moment, the conflict between our fear and our longing for freedom naturally subsides.

Birds and nature don't judge; they don't tell us how we can and can't be. The natural world is devoid of judgment. Judgments merely exist in our own minds. Watching birds

lets us be our authentic selves to let go of ideas of what we should or shouldn't do and feel. In their company, we're free to be just as we are, however we're feeling.

Giving into Life's Flow

In spring last year, I took a boat trip to the Farne Islands, off the UK's Northumberland coast. One of Sir David Attenborough's favorite wildlife spectacles, the awe-inspiring sights and sounds of large seabird colonies found there are a magnificent opportunity to let go and experience the sheer power that birds and nature can have on us and our mind. There's little room for our ego when surrounded by the deafening sound and bewildering movements of 150,000 birds.

I remember sitting on the grass on one of the islands, overwhelmed by the cacophony of sounds created by thousands of loud, lively, bickering birds. I was merely another living being in their midst, a guest on their rocky sea home. I watched the inquisitive and characterful puffins waddling up and down the rocks and leaping off cliff edges into the sea. As they threw themselves off the rocks, they clumsily dangled their bright orange webbed feet beneath them as they free fell. Graceful arctic terns filled the sky, frantically flying in all directions, letting out high-pitched screeching sounds in defense of their nests below. Razorbills and guillemots crowded the rocky ledges on the cliff sides, preening, fluttering their wings, and resting in small groups, looking out to sea. Cormorants sat on

their nests, protecting their fluffy chicks, and kittiwakes cuddled up in pairs, preening each other in the sun. Black-headed gulls joined in the general commotion wherever they were able: sitting on rocks, taking to the sky, or bobbing up and down, floating on the waves down below. All the birds were intensely animated and spirited. As I shifted my attention from one to the next, immersed in the scene, I felt increasingly excited and high on life. The separation between the birds and me dissipated. I fell into a rushing, dizzying exhilaration as I joined them in their mesmerizing dances over the island. In that moment, it was clear—the birds had shared with me the greatest gift of all: freedom.

SPREAD YOUR WINGS

Stand by the seashore. Ensure your body is upright and alert, as if a piece of string were tugging your head up toward the sky. Become aware of your feet touching the ground. Feel the sand and rocks between your toes. Enjoy the sensation of the waves as they wash over your feet and onto the shore. Once you feel grounded, lift and open up your arms into a giant T. Imagine you are a bird about to take flight over the waves. Embrace all sounds and sights around you. If any inhibitory thoughts come to mind, such as "I feel silly" or "What if people are watching me?," notice them and let them go. Just come back to the sensations of the wind on your skin and your feet on the ground. How does this posture make you feel? Close your eyes and gently repeat to yourself "I'm strong, alive, and free."

CHAPTER FOUR

EMBRACING THE SKIES

*In mountains, we find ourselves high
above the narratives of the human mind, better
able to gain perspective on our place in the web of life.
Bird watching in mountains, amid the essential forces
of nature, can be conducive to nurturing acceptance
and patience toward the uncontrollable experiences
in our lives. Birds are scarcer in mountain landscapes,
so bird watching there is an opportunity to cultivate
gratitude for the birds that we do chance to see
and hear. Acceptance, patience, and gratitude can
bring greater fulfillment in our everyday lives,
as well as when bird watching.*

WHERE EAGLES FLY

◆

Where mystical, solitary birds take to the skies, bird watching becomes a great source of wisdom; acceptance and patience are paramount when watching birds in high mountains. Nevertheless, when the conditions are right, our encounters with these elusive creatures can take our breath away.

MOUNTAIN LANDSCAPES fill me with respect and relaxed contemplation in the face of their purity and raw beauty. You can't argue with mountains. You can't avoid them or imagine they're not there. You can merely gaze up at them in reverence, as they reveal the essence of pure life. If the sea, wind, and waves help us let go, the powerful stillness of mountain landscapes is ideal when learning to acknowledge things as they really are, beyond the assessments of our minds.

◆

He clasps the crag with crooked hands;
Close to the sun in lonely lands,
Ringed with the azure world, he stands.
The wrinkled sea beneath him crawls;
He watches from his mountain walls,
And like a thunderbolt he falls.

FROM "THE EAGLE"
ALFRED, LORD TENNYSON (1809–1892)

◆

One of the most well-known mountain bird species is the golden eagle, a magnificent bird that has forever inspired great fascination in us. When walking in high mountain ranges, many of us hope to see one of these awe-inspiring creatures, soaring through the sky on broad, outspread wings. My desire to catch a glimpse of one for the first time last year taught me a lot about acceptance, patience, and gratitude and their value when bird watching.

From Expectation to Acceptance

I was on a group hiking vacation in the Austrian Alps. Every day, stunning walks organized by our hosts took us through lush valleys, dramatic canyons, beautiful pine forests, and along crashing white-water rivers. Each morning offered a new possibility that perhaps that day would bring my first encounter with a golden eagle. I was eager to experience this impressive bird, perhaps because of its traditional mystical attributes. "There are definitely eagles up here, but we're lucky if we spot one, they're rare, secretive birds," explained our hosts. I found myself regularly stopping along the path to look skyward, and soon my mind began to play tricks on me—every silhouette, be it a vulture, raven, or buzzard, was a potential golden eagle. Yet the bird continued to elude me.

By the middle of the week, I began to accept that perhaps my desire to see a golden eagle would remain unfulfilled and decided to let go of my mind's fixation on this one bird.

After all, we were in a breathtaking location, surrounded by stunning scenery and fantastic wildlife. Why dwell on what wasn't there instead of appreciating the here and now and tuning into the many other natural wonders around me?

On our next hike, I consciously brought my attention to the multitude of other birds we encountered. I noticed the bright yellow beaks of streaky brown alpine accentors and the glossy black alpine choughs in acrobatic flight. I heard the harsh calls of spotted nutcrackers in the pine trees and delighted in watching the bobbing behavior of dippers sitting on rocks in fast-flowing rivers. How could I have downgraded all these varied and wonderful creatures in favor of my golden eagle fantasy?

On the way back down the mountain that afternoon, our path took us through a steep alpine meadow dotted with rich purple gentians. After another glorious hike in the sun, we were tired and sat down for a snack before the final couple of miles back. Moments later, we heard a mournful, high-pitched hybrid between a scream and whistle echo across the valley. A small furry head rose above a tuft of grass only a few yards away: a marmot sitting up nervously on its hind legs, repeating its echoing call. A few of us began to take photographs; it was the closest view of a marmot we had had all week.

Notice what happens in your mind when unwanted thoughts occur.

"Golden eagle!," our host exclaimed, just a few seconds later. We almost dropped our cameras with excitement as the marmot momentarily lost our attention. Both dying to express our thrill yet stunned into absolute silence, we stared upward. We couldn't believe our eyes—immediately over-head, the regal, majestic master of the mountain skies was effortlessly gliding down the valley ahead of us. Not only that, it was clutching a marmot in its talons, having just snatched one off the mountainside.

THE WAY THINGS ARE

Life doesn't always go our way, yet learning to see reality with honesty is the only way to adapt to the uncontrollable challenges life can sometimes throw at us. Acceptance isn't intuitive for our controlling minds—but it's vital to our happiness and well-being.

OUR EXPERIENCE ISN'T ALWAYS AS we'd like it to be; but as we explored in chapter three, we can't control all aspects of our lives. No one wants to go through heartbreak, entertain self-critical thoughts, fail a driving test, or be criticized by other people. Notice what happens in your mind when these unwanted thoughts, emotions, and events occur. How does your mind react? Often, it will play narratives such as "I wish that hadn't happened," "Why does this always happen to me?" or "Why don't people like me?"

This narrative resistance to our unfolding experience can cause us unnecessary stress and frustration. This is because cursing unwanted experiences will never make them untrue. Instead, our mind's responses worsen an already difficult situation by creating conflict between how things are and how we want them to be. In these moments, it's important to send ourselves compassion—we've done nothing wrong. Our mind evolved with a need to control—it's simply trying to do its job as best it can. When these undesirable experiences arise, practice shifting your awareness away from your mind's reactive narratives and back to what's really happening.

On Acceptance

Acceptance isn't easy; it requires honesty and courage. It needs us to have a genuine willingness to let go of the grips of our mind. Embracing the truth of the moment is the essence of mindfulness—and acceptance is the most profound way of being in the world. It's the raw, unadulterated experience of life—the only way to meet life as it truly is.

◆

Of course there is no formula for success,
except perhaps an unconditional acceptance
of life, and what it brings.

ARTHUR RUBINSTEIN (1887–1982)
CLASSICAL PIANIST

◆

FIRST & SECOND ARROWS

The Buddha called the unavoidable pains of life "first arrows" and our reactive thoughts about them "second arrows." First arrows are unavoidable—physical and emotional pains are part of life. But condemning, judging, criticizing, hating, or denying our experience of these first arrows is like being struck by a second one.

We can't always control the first arrow. However, the second arrow is optional. You may feel angry (first arrow) when you spill coffee on your carpet and then have thoughts about always being a clumsy person (second arrow), making you feel more frustrated. Or disappointed (first arrow) because your favorite evening class has been canceled and you have thoughts such as "Why? Who canceled it? I don't like this person! I hate rescheduling!" (second arrow).

Watch out for those second arrows; they're the root of most of our day-to-day suffering. Notice the first arrow; accept it. Observe any second arrows, decide if they are helpful, and, if not, let them go.

Acceptance and letting go are two sides of the same coin. While letting go is loosening our mind's constant interpretation of our life, acceptance is being honestly curious and welcoming toward our experience as it is. It's to compassionately recognize sensations, thoughts, and feelings as they arise without seeking to avoid them or push them away.

Why is acceptance important? Because it allows for a clear view of reality, helping us take wiser action toward happiness and well-being. Why is acceptance so hard? Because the truth we see in front of us isn't always what we want to see.

INVITE YOUR EXPERIENCE TO TEA

Acceptance requires space and time. Our busy modern lives don't leave us much time to see things as they really are—away from phones, emails, and all the demands everyday life makes of us. It leaves little time for us to be aware of what's going on in our experience. But recognizing what we think and feel is important if we are to make choices to welcome happiness into our lives. Take time out to experience yourself.

When you do, invite your experience for a cup of tea. Ask yourself what is here, right now? How do I feel? Notice your thoughts, emotions, and sensations. Be curious about them. Turn toward them—learn from them—but don't get lost in them. Say to your experience: "Hi, I'm a little busy, but do come and sit with me." Hold it lightly in your awareness. Then, move on with your life. Take your thoughts, emotions, and bodily sensations with you. Be compassionate toward yourself; acceptance is hard.

Acceptance in the short term often leads to well-being in the long term. At its most basic, imagine you've started showing flu symptoms, but you have so much work that your mind harshly convinces you that you're OK and just need to keep going. You listen to your mind and plow on, ignoring how you're feeling. In doing so, you start to override your body's need to rest. You then develop a high temperature and feel worse. Your body becomes so weak and exhausted that you don't have the energy to get out of bed. Eventually, you're forced into taking three weeks off work to recover.

What if you'd initially recognized and accepted that your body was fighting a virus? Perhaps resting earlier would have enabled you to make a faster recovery.

Acceptance can also lead to greater happiness in the short term. You may be waiting for a train with a colleague to get to an important meeting. The train doesn't arrive and delays are announced. You begin to feel restless and have thoughts such as "I wish the trains weren't always late," "The people who run the trains are incompetent," or "My day is ruined."

As resistance ripens, emotions may arise, such as anger and frustration. You may find yourself trying to avoid these feelings, crushing them under your mind's monologue: "I must calm down," "What's wrong with me?," "I need to relax." If someone else is with you, you may start to vent and attempt to engage that person in your negative narratives, spreading frustration to them, too.

What if you acknowledged the situation and your restlessness? What if you compassionately recognized your frustration as normal, accepted that your mind's reactions wouldn't resolve the

Say to your experience: "Hi, I'm a little busy, but come and sit with me."

situation, but noticed a coffee shop nearby? Perhaps you could invite your friend to prepare for the meeting over a hot drink and inform your hosts of your being late? Would that not make your morning more enjoyable and productive?

Grant me the serenity to accept the things
I cannot change, the courage to change the things I can,
and the wisdom to know the difference.

FROM "THE SERENITY PRAYER"
REINHOLD NIEBUHR (1892–1971)

Strength in Active Acceptance

There's a common belief that accepting our experience is a sign of weakness and passiveness. This is not so. Acceptance isn't passive; it's active. There's an important distinction between active acceptance and passive resignation. If you're stuck in mud, passive resignation says, "Oh no, I'm stuck. Nothing I can do about it, I'll have to stay here." Acceptance says, "Oh no, I don't like it, but I'm stuck. What can I do to get unstuck?" Acceptance is not about liking or agreeing with what's happening. Nor is it about resigning yourself to how things are and giving up. Instead, it's honestly seeing what's there regardless of our mind's assessment. This is the first step that enables us to learn to change what we can and accept what we can't. This understanding is where true wisdom lies.

Be compassionate toward yourself in the practice of acceptance; our mind is extremely good at misleading us about how things truly are. To be honest with ourselves and our direct experience is the work of a lifetime. Let's now return to our feathered mountain relatives to help us on our way.

PURE, UNTOUCHED LIFE

◆

Bird watching in mountain landscapes reminds us that the natural world accepts and doesn't judge. Surrounded by pure, untouched wilderness, our mind's controlling narratives fade, having neither power nor place. Our mind quietens into an effortless acceptance and insight into the nature of reality.

SHARING A MOMENT WITH MAGELLANIC woodpeckers in the monkey puzzle forests of Chile vividly inspired in me this intangible acceptance, which I often experience in nature. These stunning birds are one of the largest woodpeckers in the world. My friends and I found some shade and stopped for a short rest after a difficult trek up the mountainside in the summer sunshine.

We sat enjoying our sandwiches among a variety of shades of green in dense bamboo, ferns, beech trees, and laurel trees. In the distance, we noticed a dotted line of motionless, bottle green parasols growing out of the mountain ridge up against the blue sky; they were monkey puzzle trees.

As we continued our hike, it wasn't long before we found ourselves surrounded by these tall evergreens, copiously adorned with soft mosses and pale green lichens. Their spiky, stiff leaves and strong branches left them immune to the wind, standing in perfect stillness. These special living fossil forests coexisted with dinosaurs in the Jurassic period. As we walked

on through this mystical, primeval world, we noticed a blinding white light in a clearing ahead. Moving closer, we discovered fresh snow—a surreal sight for us in our summer T-shirts. The farther we walked, the more snow there was, until eventually the whole forest was cloaked in an immaculate, pure white carpet, glistening in the sun.

We took another break to tune in to the absolute silence of this magical place. A few moments later, we heard a loud double drumming in the distance: "ta-dap!" The pure sound echoed in all directions through the clear, still air of the forest. We heard it again, "ta-dap," closer this time.

We walked toward its source and stopped once again, patiently waiting to see if the drummer revealed itself. Soon enough, one of my friends began to point frantically at a nearby monkey puzzle tree, struggling to contain his excitement as he tried to avoid creating disturbance. There it was, only a few feet away: a glorious Magellanic woodpecker clinging to the side of the gigantic tree trunk. Its bright red head and black body were in stark contrast to the white snow. We then saw its partner, with her curly, expressive crest on the back of her head.

As I experienced the woodpeckers' vibrant colors, the pure air, the white snow, and the complete silence, everything felt pristine and devoid of complication. These birds lived so far from the hustle and bustle of the human world. During the unforgettable ten minutes we spent watching them, time

stood still. Reality was crystal clear and authentic; there was nothing to argue with or comment on.

That evening, when we returned to our hostel and I thought back to our time in the monkey puzzle forests and

---

This being human is a guest house.

Every morning a new arrival.

A joy, a depression, a meanness,

some momentary awareness comes

as an unexpected visitor.

Welcome and entertain them all!

Even if they are a crowd of sorrows,

who violently sweep your house

empty of its furniture,

still, treat each guest honorably.

He may be clearing you out

for some new delight.

The dark thought, the shame, the malice.

meet them at the door laughing and invite them in.

Be grateful for whatever comes.

because each has been sent

as a guide from beyond.

FROM "THE GUEST HOUSE"
JALALUDDIN RUMI (1207–1273)
TRANSLATION BY COLEMAN BARKS

seeing the woodpeckers, my memory was one of immersion in a mysterious, sacred world. Life up there had seemed so remote from ours. I had huge respect for the woodpeckers' ability to survive in such harsh conditions. I'd caught a glimpse of pure, untouched life.

A Sense of Perspective

Gaining renewed perspective on our place in the world is also conducive to acceptance. Sometimes, we get so caught up in our mind's stories that we lose this sense of perspective. We see the world through the lens of our own narratives and personal dramas, which, in the grand scheme of things, don't have a rational place. The world we create in our minds is rarely a genuine reflection of reality.

Have you ever applied for a job you wanted and not got it? I once went on a weekend trip to the mountains of northern Spain a few days after failing to get a job I'd applied for. I had really wanted the job and felt deeply disappointed. When we arrived, I took a walk from our guest house, hoping that I'd left any job-related thoughts back at home. But my mind instantly returned to its angry, self-critical thinking, replaying my job interview back to me, asking what I could have done differently. It wouldn't let go of these thoughts, as if they were the most important thing in the world. I decided to take my thoughts with me on my walk. I wandered along a road spiraling up the mountainside, surrounded by rocky

peaks laden with green forests and dotted with small mountain huts. As I brought my attention to the scenery around me, the landscape was in perpetual transformation—the clouds, the light, the shadows, and all the different parts of the view were constantly changing. Every step was a new perspective.

I was struck by the scale and power of the mountains, as their spectacular slopes dropped down into the valley. As I lost myself in the vastness of the scene, my mind's narratives began to dissipate. I noticed small birds flitting across the hillsides, intermittently perching on trees and bushes. They looked minuscule, integrally part of the mountain slopes. Around the next corner, two griffon vultures were visible in the distance, circling

The world we create in our minds is rarely a genuine reflection of reality.

over the peaks on the other side of the valley. As I watched them through binoculars, they were difficult to keep track of, periodically disappearing behind a cloud or over the ridge.

I walked on farther, when suddenly I heard a loud, powerful wing flap. As I peered over the edge of the rock face, another griffon vulture appeared from below me in the valley. For a moment, the impressive bird was astoundingly close as I gazed down at it. It must have just launched itself into the air from a crag in the cliff. I was mesmerized by its majestic flight; its pale brown and black feathers, creamy white ruff, and incredible wingspan were so distinctive that they captured

MESSENGERS OF PATIENCE

Patience is an important aspect of acceptance; it's our capacity to accept delays and difficulties without agitation. Sometimes, things take time and there's nothing we can do about it. The pace of mountain life is much slower than that of our modern lives, and birds living there can be marvelous messengers of patience. Up there, it's clear that "good things come to those who wait." Whether you notice kestrels indefatigably hovering to hunt for voles until they catch their required four to seven a day, nesting dotterels sitting out treacherous snowstorms on mountaintops, or fishing herons waiting for the perfect moment to strike on low mountain lakes let yourself be inspired by the infinite patience displayed by birds.

my full attention. The mountain landscape no longer existed; all I could see was the breathtaking bird. It was a matter of seconds before he began to soar away across the valley, his silhouette blending into the landscape. Before I knew it, he was out of sight again. In that moment, I experienced a calm surrender to the power of the mountains; the unacceptable became acceptable. Like the vulture being absorbed into the landscape, my failed job interview paled into insignificance. As I brought my attention to the awe-inspiring beauty of the natural world around me, my perspective shifted. The vulture and I were part of something much greater than the contents of my mind. Our only option was to succumb to the formidable dominance of the landscape—and we both did.

Acceptance in Mindful Bird Watching

Bird watching will never yield instant gratification. It depends on acceptance and patience, and letting go of knowledge and expectations is an important part of this process. However, we can draw upon what we know to take a good guess at which birds we will probably encounter at certain times in certain places. The likelihood of encountering a griffon vulture in high mountains is much greater than meeting one in your yard! We can estimate our chances of finding a particular bird species based on our knowledge of its biology, how common it is, the time of year it's normally present, and its habitat. This information is invaluable for understanding and protecting birds and nature. Nevertheless, when it comes to mindful bird watching, we can learn to go beyond it.

If birds are individual living beings and not stimulus-response machines, meeting a particular bird at a given point in time will depend on the behavior of the bird in that moment. This applies wherever we are, but it's particularly relevant to mountain bird watching. In these landscapes, many birds, such as my avidly hoped-for golden eagle, are less abundant. Farthermore, birds that live in the mountains are subject to rapid changes in weather conditions, making them more difficult to find. This means that we must be prepared for the fact that our expectations of coming across a snowy owl, a bald eagle, a bluethroat, or a yellow wagtail won't always be met.

Chance Encounters

Although this can be frustrating, the fact that we can't always predict birds can also be a wonderful source of excitement, anticipation, and possibility. What birds will we come across? Where will we see them? What will they be doing? Nature is full of wonder, because it's variable, surprising, and always changing. The unpredictability of bird watching and the unexpected beauty we find in our moments with birds is what makes mindful bird watching so magnificent and rewarding.

Through the practice of mindful acceptance, our chance encounters with birds become gifts. I felt immensely grateful for my experiences with the Magellanic woodpeckers, the golden eagle, and the vultures. Mountain bird watching can

---

MOUNTAIN BIRD-WATCHING MEDITATION

As you walk, notice expectations you may be holding about what birds you may meet, observe them, and let them go. Bring your awareness back to sights and sounds in the landscape. Open up to the unexpected in each moment—and accept the possibility of seeing no birds at all. Notice how you respond. Do you feel boredom? Disappointment? Anticipation? Compassionately welcome your responses as they arise—they are perfectly normal. Then let them go and return to what you can see and hear. Welcome any birds you come across. Give them your full attention, whatever they are and whatever they're doing. And let them go as they return to blend into the landscape again.

---

spontaneously inspire gratitude, perhaps due to the heightened contrast between seeing nothing at all and suddenly encountering the elusive creatures that live amid the vastness of the landscape. We can learn to nurture this gratitude more actively in bird watching as in everyday life.

GRATEFUL FOR LIFE

Cultivating gratitude is the ideal antidote to our mind's negativity bias, which can otherwise leave us with a persistent feeling of dissatisfaction. Why? Because whatever we have, our mind will focus on what's not going well and constantly tell us that we need more.

EXPERIENCING GRATITUDE counteracts our mind's craving, controlling habits. We can develop gratitude the way we can develop any skill, such as cooking or learning a musical instrument. Gratitude is becoming aware of what we do have instead of dwelling on what we don't. It isn't a moral imperative or a dutiful thank you. It's an act of self-compassion. Simply, feeling grateful makes us happier.

Bring to mind a recent experience you enjoyed. Notice how recalling it makes you feel. Does it make you smile? Does it instill a sense of warmth and satisfaction? The fact is, experiencing and expressing gratitude makes us feel good. Recent research has shown that gratitude can have strong links to enhanced well-being and fulfillment and makes us feel

---

MINDFULNESS EXERCISE

CULTIVATING GRATITUDE

Every evening, write down three things that went well that day, that you appreciated and are grateful for, be it your hot cup of coffee in the morning, the moments you shared with birds on your lunch break, or something kind someone said to you—we have many simple things to feel grateful for. Recalling them each day is an easy practice to enhance our feelings of happiness and satisfaction.

---

more fully alive. Science also demonstrates that the more we practice, the more we change the programming of our brains to automatically focus on what's going well in our lives. Through regular practice, gratitude becomes an attitude of mind—a receptive and open welcoming of our experience, whatever it brings. In mindful bird watching, gratitude and acceptance go hand in hand.

A Precious Trio

Torrent ducks live on fast-flowing rivers, high up in the mountains. I once discovered a family of them sitting on a rock in a fast-flowing glacial mountain stream in Patagonia. At the time, I didn't know they were in the area; the wild, raging water didn't seem like it would support much birdlife.

I was astonished when I saw the intrepid trio huddled together on the rock amid the powerful white water rushing down the mountain. The female was a beautiful red-orange color with a gray back and head. Her striking, bright red bill matched her partner's in his stunning, distinctive black, white, and gray streaks. Their colors were brilliantly pristine, as if purified by the high mountain air and clear water. Between them sat their one and only chick, patiently waiting for its attentive parents to dive in for more invertebrates and mollusks to eat. Watching the three of them was incredibly special and humbling. Bringing this memory to mind makes me smile and I'm reminded that being alive is unbelievably precious—there's so much to be grateful for.

Both abundance and lack exist simultaneously
in our lives, as parallel realities. It is always our
conscious choice which secret garden we will tend . . .
When we choose not to focus on what is missing from
our lives but are grateful for the abundance that's
present—love, health, family, friends, work, the joys of
nature, and personal pursuits that bring us pleasure—
the wasteland of illusion falls away and
we experience heaven on earth.

FROM "SIMPLE ABUNDANCE"
SARAH BAN BREATHNACH

CHAPTER FIVE

ON THE WINGS
OF WISDOM

As we deepen our relationship
with birds, wherever we are in the world,
we'll start to become sensitive to seasonal changes
in their wonderful colors, beautiful songs, and
mysterious behaviors. Twice a year, we may notice
the arrivals and departures of some of them, as they
undertake their extraordinary migrations. Birds are
excellent reminders of the passing of time, daily
teachers of the undeniable impermanence of life.
For this reason, bird watching can be a profound
source of wisdom for us all.

MESSENGERS OF SEASONAL CHANGE

◆

Birds across the globe are constantly responding to seasonal changes in temperature, light, and rainfall. Whether they're responding to the four seasons in temperate regions or to the dry and rainy seasons in the tropics, birds are excellent messengers of seasonal change.

SWALLOWS AND HOUSE MARTINS were wheeling around over the rooftops, catching insects as they do on every summer's day. But where were the swifts? I'd been away from my office window vantage point for a week and something was missing. The swifts had gone—taken to the skies on their monumental six-thousand-mile southerly migration. It was mid-August and their absence starkly marked the beginning of the end of summer, or should I say the start of fall?

It's always with sadness that I notice the swifts' departure; the exaltation in their twirling flight against clear blue skies is the most glorious celebration of the height of summer. However, their disappearance is also the cue for the exciting anticipation of the unpredictable to come. As we grieve the loss of our summer visitors on the move south to warmer climes, we welcome our winter visitors from the north embarking on their southbound migrations. From songbirds to waterfowl to birds of prey, millions of birds migrate across the United States, sometimes resting at stopping points along the way. Amid this colossal global changeover, unusual

things occur. Some winter visitors arrive early and some summer visitors stay later. Unfortunate vagrant birds sometimes turn up when blown off course from their usual migration routes, gifting us a thrilling glimpse of the exotic.

The withdrawal of the swifts is also the prelude for all other autumnal delights to follow. Fresh dew, mature fall colors, golden afternoon light, and blustery, constantly changing equinox weather are all on their way as our loyal, resident birds prepare themselves for the cold winter ahead, with their changing colors, songs, and behaviors.

Change is bittersweet. It's exhilarating, concerning, and relieving. It sparks sadness and joy. It provokes resistance toward the unknown and powerful desire to hold onto the past. It brings both exciting transformation and nostalgia for what has been and gone. Throughout the year, mindful bird watching lets us perpetually experience natural change. Whether watching birds at home, in open country and forests, by the sea or in mountains, we hardly need our calendars to know that fall has arrived.

Matters of Time

Birds live on nature's time; their lives depend on continual fluctuations in food and water availability, temperature, and light. Like all living creatures, they've evolved to maximize their chances of staying alive to raise the next generation. For this reason, they breed in the spring, when food sources are fresh and plentiful. At this time of the year, they're able to attract partners, build nests, and defend safe territories—leaving them enough time to nurture their young before winter returns. When fall arrives, birds begin to prepare for the cold months ahead. Some migrate, traveling huge distances to find food elsewhere, while others have developed strategies to be sure they have sufficient supplies to keep them alive during freezing winter temperatures. During this challenging season, many birds depend heavily on our backyard feeders until spring returns.

If time matters to birds, then it's equally important to bird watchers, with each season bringing something different—new sights and sounds for our attention. What seasonal changes can we look and listen out for in the avian world?

CONNECTING WITH NATURAL RHYTHMS

Wherever we live in the world, the bird species we encounter—as well as their colors, songs and behaviors—will change throughout the seasons. As you embark on your mindful bird-watching journey, notice which birds you can see at different times of year. Do some of them become more or less numerous? Can you hear different calls and songs? Do you notice any changes in their plumage? How do their behaviors change? As you tune into the changes of our avian friends, let the birds connect you with the rhythms of the natural world.

Explosion of Life

Every year, it's always with great elation that I see my first swallow back after its long journey from sub-Saharan Africa, proclaiming with gusto that spring has officially returned. It's a delight to watch it as it gleefully teases the river surface, catching insects on the wing. New life is coming and the swifts, too, will soon return to join in the celebration.

Spring is the natural festival of life, and birds are undoubtedly the stars of the show. Have you noticed that many of our winged companions show off much brighter colors at this time of year? Shiny, glossy blackbirds, dazzling yellow American goldfinches, brilliant orange-billed puffins, and stunning tortoiseshell-patterned turnstones all parade their pristine breeding plumage to be sure they attract the perfect partner.

Robins, wrens, blackbirds, warblers, chickadees, and wood thrushes complement this vibrant courtship carnival with their captivating frenzy of loud song—powerfully broadcasting their morning tunes, while avidly defending their territories against intruders. Be sure to spend at least one early morning out in woodland, fully immersed in the

Spring is the natural festival
of life and birds are undoubtedly
the stars of the show.

spellbinding cacophony of the spring dawn chorus. Other birds, including drumming snipe, booming bitterns, and whistling redshanks, use special calls to attract their mates, while eagles, buzzards, and vultures perform their stunning display dives and glides to woo their partners. Puffins, gannets, razorbills, and guillemots gather in gigantic colonies to breed. Wherever we are, spring is simply a wonderful time to watch birds—a time to feel intensely alive, part of the magnificent annual replenishment of the natural world.

Summer Tranquillity

When summer comes, a sense of peace and quietening descends and our avian soundtrack is reduced to a few soft tweets and chirps. Most birds are saving their energy to tend their nests and search for food for their young. Look for demanding young fledglings as many continue to beg for food.

How do these geese know when to fly to the sun?
Who tells them the seasons? How do we, humans,
know when it is time to move on? As with the migrant
birds, so surely with us, there is a voice within, if only
we would listen to it, that tells us so certainly when
to go forth into the unknown.

FROM "THE WHEEL OF LIFE"
ELISABETH KÜBLER-ROSS (1926–2004)

You may see them next to their parents, perched with mouth agape, wings quivering, eagerly awaiting that extra mouthful.

Just as we begin to relax in to this tranquil time of natural respite, we realize the swifts have disappeared again. Soon after, the swallows are darting around, anxiously gathering on telephone wires, seemingly apprehensive about their six-week-long journey south. Fall is on its way once again.

Times of Change

As the robins' upbeat spring tunes turn weak and wistful, it becomes clear that fall has arrived. Despite the melancholic resonance of their song as they grieve the passing of summer, I'm comforted in the knowledge that our characterful companions will sing us all the way through the winter. Look for them and their vibrant red breasts; let them brighten any cold, bleak winter days. Robins are one of those few species that broadcast their songs all year round.

The robins' mournful tones are mirrored by the molting of many birds into subdued color shades. It's as if the intense exuberance of spring leaves the essential vitality of life in need of a well-deserved rest. You may notice that small birds such as goldfinches, orioles, and Northern cardinals appear faded and lackluster. Black-headed gulls and terns shed their distinguished black caps and puffins lose their striking orange beaks. Molting buzzards, golden eagles, and vultures turn ragged, giving them an ever so slightly less dignified appearance than usual.

Meanwhile, titmice, wrens, and chickadees are beginning to group into large flocks for safety and warmth in numbers, especially when the trees begin to shed the leaves that usually provide the birds with hiding places from hungry predators. Within these flocks, you may see other birds sneaking into the crowd to reap the benefits, including goldcrests, nuthatches and cardinals. In fall, the starlings will launch into their must-see murmuration spectacles and their transfixing aerial ballets.

In all temperate regions of the northern hemisphere, fall is also a time when we welcome migrant birds traveling from colder northern climes to spend the winter with us. Thrushes, finches, blackbirds, robins, and starlings that spent the spring farther north toward the Arctic will join our resident birds at this time of year. You may want to welcome these visitors by leaving your fruit, berries and seed-bearing plants in your yard into late fall.

Holding On Through Winter

When winter descends with its icy cold spells, it becomes increasingly tough for birds to find enough food and water to maintain warmth and energy reserves. It's for this reason that nuthatches will hoard acorns in the fall months, burying them underground and recovering them in snowy winters, thanks to their incredible spatial memory. Winter is also a time when a freshwater bath and a well-stocked bird feeder is absolute paradise for our backyard visitors. At this time of year, more

THE MIRACLE OF MIGRATION

Extraordinary distances

Did you know that many birds undertake awe-inspiring journeys twice a year in search of food and territories? It's not fully understood how, but birds appear to use the sun, stars, and the earth's magnetic force as their compasses. These long-distance migrants include wildfowl, waders, seabirds, raptors, swifts, swallows, martins, and warblers. Arctic terns hold the distance record of flying more than 59,000 miles (95,000 km) from their breeding grounds in the Farne Islands (on the northeast coast of England) to Antarctica and back again.

Why do birds migrate?

Birds that nest in the northern hemisphere travel northward in the spring. Here, they find plenty of space to nest and fewer predators. They also find longer daylight hours during which to feed their young, and food is plentiful, with a lot of insects and budding plants. When winter is on its way in the north, the availability of food drops, and the birds move south again, where the supply of insects is often plentiful all year round.

Enjoying the wonder of migration

Notice the signs of bird migration. Spot the tremendous flocks of ducks, geese, and waders as they arrive for the winter. Celebrate the return of the swallows and swifts. Enjoy the spring tunes of warblers back from their warmer winter breaks and spare a moment of compassion in fall for the jittering swallows, anxiously preparing for their long journeys south again.

than any other, it's important to make sure you keep your bird feeder well filled, because our feathered relatives will really depend on it. And as you trudge out to fill up your bird feeder on a winter's morning, perhaps spare a well-wishing thought for our prodigious long-distance travelers, hoping they're safe in their warmer winter destinations.

Solace in Cycles

As birds reconnect us with the bittersweet nature of change, they also remind us of the comfort there is in the cyclical essence of natural change. Is there not reassurance in realizing that although they have come and gone, the familiar sights and sounds of our avian companions will return next year? We will experience the outburst of spring song, the humble nest building, and the fledging of young birds once again. And when we do, we may sense that whatever's going on in our lives, all must be well with the world, as nature continues to sustain the miracle of life. The swifts had disappeared from my office window view, but they would be back next year, toasting the summer, circling high in dazzling blue skies.

◆

Nothing endures but change.

Heraclitus (ca. 535–ca. 475 bce)
Greek Philosopher

◆

THE IMPERMANENCE OF LIFE

◆

Mindful bird watching is a constant reminder of the passing of time, with all the hope, anticipation, excitement, grief, and nostalgia that it brings. Life is transient, fluid, and evanescent; things are always changing. This is what the Buddha called the "impermanence" of life.

Impermanence isn't a theory or a belief—it's simply an essential property of all natural processes and life forms. We're an integral part of the natural world and so can directly observe impermanence within ourselves and around us every single day of our lives. As our awareness grows, it's indisputable that nothing is permanent; thoughts, emotions, events, relationships —and ultimately life itself—are all destined to change or end at some point.

For us, as conscious human beings, impermanence is a double-edged sword. If everything perpetually changes, we know that pain doesn't persist forever, which gives us hope. However, it also means that all we cherish will one day fade. The thought that we may lose what we love, enjoy, and value can be deeply unsettling. Sometimes, it can even throw our whole lives into question, including the choices we've made and the things we've given priority to. Nevertheless, however we feel about the impermanence of our lives, there's absolutely nothing we can do about this undeniable fact of existence. For better or for worse, everything will pass.

In Harmony with Life

We've explored how much effort we invest in living in the realm of our minds—cursing impermanence, pushing away unwanted experiences, and longing for what we desire. But when we open up to the reality of life, it becomes clear that these habits cause most of our unnecessary suffering beyond life's unavoidable pains. Put simply, the majority of the suffering we experience happens entirely within our own minds.

Our minds have naturally evolved to crave for things to be stable, permanent, and substantial. But in reality, the natural world—with all the life it sustains—is impermanent, fluid, and interconnected. With this insight, it becomes clear that many of the controlling narratives of our minds are entirely futile and potentially damaging. Why create so much frustration, anxiety, and suffering for ourselves by living in conflict with the natural world we're part of? What if, instead, we saved our energy for living in cooperation with life?

Mindfulness cynics often state: "I'm not really 'into' mindfulness. I don't need it." But mindfulness isn't a hobby or a therapy. It's simply the awareness we can nurture to learn to live in tune with the natural flow of the world. Mindfulness gives us the power to end our perpetual conflict with the nature of reality within us and around us and to live in harmony with life. Once we start to pay attention, mindfulness becomes intuitively appropriate when it comes to happiness and well-being—for ourselves and for the natural world.

Moreover, if life is impermanent, we can only live one moment at a time. Each one is the only opportunity we have to direct our attention, make choices, and take action—anything else is mere fantasy of the mind. Welcome the moment, come to your senses, let go of your mind's unhelpful narratives, and accept life as it unfolds. Practice as often as you can. Ask yourself, "What is my experience right now?" and gratefully receive whatever you find. In each moment, there is joy and peace—if we choose to shine the light of our awareness wisely. Therein lies the secret of happiness for us all.

The Whole World in the Eyes of an Owl

One of my most insightful, treasured bird-watching experiences occurred at dawn, in the middle of the swamp forests of Cuba, where I was looking for Cuban todies. Although I'd seen them on various occasions during my Cuban travels, I hoped I might have been gifted with a few more moments in their charming company before getting my flight home the following day. A few minutes into my walk, I heard their delightfully distinctive "tut-tut-tut-tut" calls around me, amid the irksome whining sound of mosquitoes. Still, I struggled to see them through the dense forest. Eventually, the heat, the mosquitoes, and the lack of todies challenged my patience, leaving me unreasonably frustrated. Reminding myself that birds don't turn up on demand, I decided to turn back, grateful for at least having heard the todies once again.

As I followed the path back to my lodge, I turned a corner and suddenly found myself face to face with a pygmy owl, perched on a branch only two or three feet away. A stunning apparition. The noble bird stared straight at me through astonishing bright yellow eyes. Its gaze expressed a mysterious combination of piercing wildness and total serenity. As we looked into each other's eyes—during what felt like a fleeting, yet infinite moment—the first ray of sunshine of the day filtered through the trees and lit up the top of his beautiful brown-and-white speckled head. Together, we welcomed the sunlight in complete stillness.

This was the enthralling silence of the wild. For a moment, all noise stopped, be it the chatter of my mind or the whining mosquitoes. I saw reality with intense clarity, as I lost myself in the owl's stare. I was left in awe, with respect, humility, and

◆

This is a sacred and connected silence.
It's like a deep, still pond reflecting the stars
of the night sky. I believe this is the baseline for
human consciousness, and I'm convinced that
the birds are the best mentors in the natural
world for bringing us to it.

FROM "WHAT THE ROBIN KNOWS:
HOW BIRDS REVEAL THE SECRETS OF THE NATURAL WORLD"
JON YOUNG

◆

absolute compassion. The bird and I became part of one another—we were no longer two separate beings. One of life's deepest truths had revealed itself; each moment is a unique set of interconnected conditions coming together for a once in a lifetime union—we call it our present experience. This wasn't about me, the owl, the sunlight, or the forest. It was about everything we shared in an unforgettable instant. Through the mesmerizing silence that had emerged between the owl and me, I had caught a glimpse of the whole world.

FOR THE LOVE OF BIRDS

What if we woke up to a world devoid of birdsong? What if the swifts and swallows didn't return next year? What if robins disappeared forever? How could we live without the comfort and joy inspired by our feathered natural relatives?

A REPORT PRODUCED BY NATIONAL AUDUBON SOCIETY in 2016 revealed that since 1966 the numbers of wintering North American bird populations has declined by about 30 per cent. The North American Bird Conservation Initiative also reported in 2016 that more than one-third of North American birds are considered at risk of extinction. During the same period, long-distance European migrant birds declined by 23 per cent. Meanwhile, there has been a steady and continuing deterioration in the status of the world's birds over the last twenty-five

years, with one in eight of all bird species considered threatened with extinction. These worrying figures are primarily the result of unsustainable agriculture, invasive species, and habitat loss, including deforestation. Unfortunately, the prospect of a world without birds is increasingly a possibility rather than a fantasy.

As we reach the end of our mindful bird-watching journey together, it is my hope that the thought of having fewer birds in our lives is a deeply devastating one for us all. A world without birds, their diversity and wisdom, is a world without beauty, a world without life. Not only do birds have an intrinsic, equal right to live their lives in our shared nature home but we need them, now more than ever.

Since the dawn of humanity, birds have inspired infinite beauty, happiness, and wisdom. They're one of our strongest connections to our natural home and so to life and to reality itself. Moreover, they're an integral part of the interconnected, delicately balanced, impermanent web that sustains all life. To lose birds is to lose a vital part of life's tapestry—and it isn't something we can afford in the context of this environmental crisis. What we do to birds, we do to ourselves and the whole of life.

Fall in Love with Birds

It's clear that the only chance we have of saving life on our planet lies in a long-term change in human behavior, based on a greater respect for the natural world we live in. I believe that it's only through nurturing a love for birds and the rest of

nature that we'll be inspired to take action to protect them. Instead of rational arguments, gloomy statistics, and scare-mongering facts, it's the magic of our experiences with birds, the wisdom and wonder they ignite in us, that are the most powerful drivers of behavioral change. We protect what we love. Our moments with birds have the power not only to heal our hearts but also to inspire us to heal our natural home.

I hope that your mindful bird-watching journey will continue after you turn this last page of this book. Mindful bird watching is a lifelong practice—fall in love with birds every day and share that love with as many other people as you can. Our world desperately needs many more of our wondrous moments of communion with birds.

What we do to birds, we do to ourselves and the whole of life.

Be compassionate toward the warblers in your yard, watch the ducks in the park through a child's eyes, celebrate the diversity of birds' colors and songs in country and forests, dance with terns over the waves, and embrace mountain skies on the accepting wings of eagles. Receive their wisdom and soar with their freedom. And you can always be certain that whatever is going on in your life, high up above the clouds, another bird has opened its wings and dared to claim the sky. In each moment, you are free to do the same.

BIBLIOGRAPHY

◆

The Poetry of Birds, Simon Armitage and Tim Dee (Penguin Books, London, 2011)

Simple Abundance, A Daybook of Comfort and Joy by Sarah Ban Breathnach (Grand Central Publishing, 2009)

How to be a Bad Birdwatcher: to the Greater Glory of Life, Simon Barnes (Short Books Ltd, London, 2012)

Bird Sense: What it's Like to be a Bird, Tim Birkhead (Bloomsbury Paperbacks, London, 2013)

The Web of Life: A New Scientific Understanding of Living Systems, Fritjof Capra (Anchor Books, New York, 1996)

The Compassionate Mind, Paul Gilbert (Constable and Robinson Ltd, London, 2013)

The Happiness Trap, Russ Harris (Constable and Robinson Ltd, London, 2008)

Life With Full Attention, Maitreyabandhu (Windhorse Publications Ltd, Cambridge, 2011)

Collins Bird Guide: The Most Complete Field Guide to the Birds of Britain and Europe, Lars Svensson, Killian Mullarney, Dan Zetterstrom, Peter J. Grant (Collins, London, 2010)

Bill Oddie's Little Black Bird Book, Bill Oddie (Eyre Methuen, London, 1980)

The North American Bird Guide, David Sibley (Pica Press, Sussex, 2000)

Happiness and How It Happens: Finding Contentment Through Mindfulness, The Happy Buddha, "Suryacitta" (Ivy Press, 2011)

Zen Mind, Beginner's Mind, Informal Talks on Zen Meditation and Practice, Shunryu Suzuki (Shambhala Publications, Boston, 2011)

Mindfulness & the Natural World: Bringing our Awareness Back to Nature, Claire Thompson (Ivy Press, 2013)

Excerpts from *What the Robin Knows: How Birds Reveal the Secrets of the Natural World* by Jon Young. Copyright © 2012 by Jon Young. Used by permission of Jon Young and Houghton Mifflin Harcourt Publishing Company. All rights reserved.

WEBSITES

◆

American Bird Conservancy: www.abcbirds.org

American Birding Association: www.aba.org

BirdLife International: www.birdlife.org

Bird Watcher's Digest: www.birdwatchersdigest.com

National Audubon Society: www.audubon.org

North American Bird Conservation Initiative: www.nabci-us.org

Royal Society for the Protection of Birds (RSPB): www.rspb.org.uk

Mindfulness of Nature: mindfulness-of-nature.com

INDEX

DEDICATION & ACKNOWLEDGMENTS

◆

To my Grandma Merle, in memory of her infinite kindness.

Thank you to all my friends and family for their unwavering support, encouragement, love, and enthusiasm as I wrote this book. Special thanks go to my wonderful proofreaders: Mom, Chris, David, Jeremy, and Jon. I couldn't have achieved this without you all.

I am immensely grateful to Monica Perdoni for giving me the amazing opportunity to write another book, which I hope will inspire many to rekindle a love and care for birds and our beautiful natural world at a time when the world desperately needs it.